INFECTED INTELLECTS

JOURNEY INTO THE KINGDOM OF I

BY
DILLEN STEEBY

 www.trafford.com

North America & international
toll-free: 1 888 232 4444 (USA & Canada)
phone: 250 383 6864 ♦ fax: 812 355 4082

This, my first published work and the beginning of the fulfillment of a dream; the realization of my potential being manifest into the real, is dedicated in loving memory of my Mom; Jeanne Sue Furgison-Steeby and my Brother; David Matthew Steeby. I miss you both every day.

I thank my Dad; Floyd Dillen Steeby: I am proud to have you as my father and my friend.

To my Son; Jordan Xavier Steeby: Pay attention Son because I want you to see that if you have a dream and you work for it you can do it.

I thank God for the gift of life and the knowledge of free will which is the truth of salvation.

CONTENTS

1. WELCOME TO THE JOURNEY   1
2. CULTURE DIFFUSION IN INTERNATIONAL HUMAN RIGHTS AND HUMAN RELATIONS   11
3. NEUROTIC CULTURE   18
4. ABRAHAM MASLOW   21
5. SELF-ACTUALIZATION OF THE CAVEMAN   25
6. WALKING THE PATH OF GOD   28
7. SOBERING THOUGHTS   30
8. SAFETY NEEDS   34
9. ESTEEM, BELONGINGNESS AND LOVE   37
10. THE HUMAN ANIMAL vs. THE HUMAN BEING   39
11. SELF-ACTUALIZING PEOPLE; HUMANS BEING   43
12. CREATIONS OF SOCIETY   51
13. BEING AN INDIVIDUAL   55
14. THE WILL TO KILL   57
15. LOVE IN SELF-ACTUALIZING PEOPLE   59
16. INDIVIDUAL RIGHTS AND CRIMINALITY   66
17. GUN CONTROL AND INDIVIDUAL RIGHTS   70
18. UNDERSTANDING 9/11 AND ITS IMPLICATIONS   78

19. CONSERVITIVE, LIBERAL OR SOMETHING
     DIFFERENT   82
20. DEATH AND OTHER CIRCUMSTANCES   86
21. IT'S NOT MUCH OF A LIFE, BUT IT IS MINE   89
22. SOME RANDOM THOUGHTS ALONG THE WAY   105
23. THANK YOU   109
24. BIBLIOGRAPHY   111

WELCOME TO THE JOURNEY

I began this project out of a lifelong desire not only to write, but to do something I feel is significant as a contribution to all mankind. I'm no doctor or professor or otherwise described as an expert in any field. I hold no degrees yet, though I soon will have completed a double bachelor's degree in the field of criminal justice, with emphasis on administration as well as law enforcement. I will probably go to work on a master's degree in international law or relations and am considering the possibility of attaining a doctorate in this field or perhaps in a field of human science; medical, psychological or perhaps genetics.

This book isn't based upon any pure research of my own in that I have conducted no empirical studies or experiments and have collected no data of my own to come up with some new idea. It can be described as a sort of guide to self-actualization. It is that while it is also a sort of layman's guide to understanding a perspective I have developed for myself through my studies of data and analysis of the work of people who have done the work of a researcher to find an understanding of the condition of being human mixed with my own thoughts based upon my experiences and insights I have found in the world around me along with my education and experience as a Christian. It is an attempt to take some massive amount of information and boil it down to the bare bones of what it truly means and try to convey it in a way that it can be easily understood by the average person. I am including perspectives from many disciplines of human studies and showing the connections between them which prove points and paint a picture of the world as I have seen it through the eye of my mind.

This is the beginning of a work and a message which I will continue to expand upon in the future as I am able to. I hope that it will be a beginning for you and me of a useful relationship. The foundation of any relationship is exchange; the sharing of some kind of resource between two entities whether it be something of a tangible nature such as food, shelter and money or intangible things such as knowledge or social satisfactions. It's not what you have in this life that matters most; it's the pieces of you that are left behind when you are but a ghost. I hope that you enjoy this little work of mine and find something to take from it which is useful to you and you can call it your own.

The Kingdom of I is a realization of oneself as a single entity which exists for its own purpose and owes its responsibility to only itself first and foremost; it is to say simply that I was born a single being and I will die a single being and my relationship to the world in which I live is as a single being. Some of my brethren of the Christian faith will argue that the purpose of human life is to serve a relationship with God, but my argument with this idea is that God's hope in our creation is, I agree, to serve a purpose of companionship, but it isn't demanded. If God wanted a being to be a companion he could have created such a being and not given them the free will to choose whether or not to be his companion. Free will is necessary because unless we are beings with a choice to choose otherwise then we are no better than robots or slaves. So God therefore created us with our own right to determine what we should be. So I am a single entity who owes nothing to anyone for what I am and no one owes me anything for it either. Everything else in life of any form of matter may be added to or taken away from me at any given moment; there are no promises or guaranties in life but birth and death. From this perspective one can begin to understand all possibility of what one can and should become through one's own examination. One can begin to know and understand the truth of life and forge their own identity through their own intent. Each of us is a single being which is the King and god of our own single universe with the power to choose what we should and can become. Each of us must decide for ourselves what is important to our existence and strengthen our resolve to take responsibility for our own lives. We must determine where we are and where we want to be and begin to design the structure which will get us from point A to point B. This is where most of us fall short in pursuit of our dreams; we fail to create a plan which will hold up to the tests of life. The world is an unforgiving place and a single lie spoken in a time of stress and immaturity can change the potential of your life.

People speak of finding yourself but it isn't about finding; it is about becoming or creating who you are. I have pieced together this idea of not a map but a sort of compass which measures the energies of reality to give one the means to understand where they truly are. Or perhaps it is a device which improves the vision so that one can see things which may have been hidden before. Like climbing to a high ground where you can see further and get a lay of the land around you so you can determine where you want to go. However you wish to define its function, I leave it to you to decide as I have no control over how you will interpret what I have done. I can only do my best to explain and define my intent and hope that you will understand my message it as it is intended.

This is the critical flaw of this tool of communication we call language; no matter the intent of my message you will draw your own interpretation as you are able to understand it. In a perfect world we wouldn't need to rely on such an inefficient means of sharing information; we could just think a thought with all its meaning and intents and pass it on in a perfect state to another without any concern for the interpretation as it would be interpreted just as it is meant. It is however the best we have available to us despite all our advances over the animals of the world our ability to communicate with one another isn't too far removed from them and in some examples far less effective; nevertheless it is all I have so I shall do the best I can with it. Hopefully someday soon someone will design a device which does everything a cell phone and personal computer can do and is small enough to be implanted at the base of my skull and be wired to my brain; then maybe I can share a perfect thought with someone else who had the device as well. There are really three intents I suppose if I must count them, yet they are only parts of a single greater intent. They are means to an end I suppose although to me the means are in and of themselves ends. So it is with careful thought and deliberation I seek to share my thoughts and intents and hope you will understand them just as I have meant. When it is done I expect I may be revered by some and demonized by others for what I have said in this work. I have no fear of the matter because I understand the truth of the message and its origin. Truth is good and deception is evil; so if my message is truth then it is of no evil and those who would try to demonize me for the truth I speak are therefore deceived or being deceptive and act out of evil by their own ignorance of intent and I will not fear evil. My experience has taught me that most people and their intentions aren't evil at all; it's just the methods they use to go about getting the job done which are questionable as being potentially evil. This is why the means are in and of themselves ends because they can cause a condition or set a thing in motion which takes on a life of its own.

A good example of the way a thing which was intended to serve one type of purpose can take on a life of its own and serve an entirely unintended side effect is Facebook. A gentleman in San Diego recently spoke out to try to convince people to stop using Facebook because he claims it causes a narcissistic condition to society. His idea is wrong-headed because his logic is backwards. I understand what he is getting at though because I have been quite dismayed at some of the things people have posted and the frequency with which they post. It seems as though some people can't go to the bathroom without letting the world know about it. The website isn't the cause of one's condition; the condition already existed in the person and they are acting out in an available forum as a result of their pre-existing condition. Simply put, the narcissist is taking advantage of the availability of a potential source of attention. The founders and creators of Facebook didn't intend to serve the narcissist, they were trying to create a way for normal average people to keep in touch with each other to build and maintain relationships, share culture and help bring people together in a world that is often too busy for us to make the time to nurture these relationships by another means. I'm not saying Facebook is a bad thing or that anything needs to be done about it. It is what it is and I find it useful for the very reasons I just mentioned, but it has found its ills from a particular type of personality. Facebook isn't causing people to be narcissists; people become what they are based upon their own choices. It's the same thing as XBOX. Hey we can play video game with people from all over the world and from all walks of life and it is great fun, but throw some of the wrong kind of people in the mix and it can be a nasty place and some people are addicts to video games as well. It's not the fault of Microsoft if someone cannot manage their own life and habits of gameplay.

The first intent is to share information and understanding. Unfortunately Abraham Maslow's work is not among popular literature and is rather difficult to find. I say it is unfortunate because it is my strong opinion that work of such wonderfully enlightening information should be found in greater quantity and in greater forum than it is. Some of his explanations, which I have been fortunate enough to be educated enough to understand may be difficult for the average reader to manage due to the nature of changes in language over time. So I wanted to bring his work and the work of others from whom I have found wisdom into a more readily understood terminology and explanation so that the average reader of average mind could well understand and be able to make use of the information as well as hopefully broaden the availability of this information. It has always been a primary goal of mine in all my writing for as long as I can remember to try my best to deliver a message which is easily understood by the average reader. I have always been somewhat irritated with modern writers who choose to use language patterns which are confusing or altogether incomprehensible to the layman. I believe it may be their desire to edify themselves which leads them to do this and it is a source of division among people. I can give them the benefit of the doubt and say they communicate the way they communicate as a matter of how they learned to communicate, but I feel it necessary to point out to them that it is important to consider your audience or potential audience when delivering your message and I would hope to somehow convince them of the necessity to not divide themselves and their work from people in this way. I would expect an educated person to come to this logical conclusion and make an effort to present their ideas in a more readily understood lingo for all people of all backgrounds. If the purpose of the educated in doing research and passing on information found in that research isn't to educate those who are unaware of that information then what purpose does it serve? Anytime you use a style of language which isn't easily understood by the majority you separate yourself and your thought and work from other human beings and limit not only yourself to sharing news with those who already know but limit others who don't know to ignorance. A good example on the other end of the spectrum which may be more easily identified is the text-speak and slang rich communication patterns of today's youth. They speak a language which is of their own design and while I can appreciate it for what it is, I think it is important for them to remember to use the normal English language they have been taught when wishing to share information with an audience which may not understand their popular speech. I do think it can be a beautiful thing; these variant language patterns, but they can become a stumbling block if they aren't managed wisely. I understand it is a tool of culture identification and as such holds a certain importance in its own context, but utilized in a different forum it creates a problem. If I went on an extended trip to Mexico and was to be there for a while I would have to learn to speak the language if I hoped to get along well with the locals there. It is the same notion with these fore mentioned language patterns. If you are going to publish a work and offer it to the general population then you should try your best to put aside your academic language patterns and adopt a language style which is better understood by the average person in your audience. I will admit that I am not perfect in this respect myself because my thought patterns aren't very readily understood by the average person which is why I do so much explaining and use analogies which I believe or at least hope will show the point I'm trying to make. If you do have a question regarding something I have written I will be happy to hear about it and will do my best to try to address it.

The second intent is to make contact with people like myself who find that their life and who they are or who they want to be is something rather different from the average person. People like me who have had difficulty adjusting to normal society or culture all their life and as a consequence may feel as though something is wrong with them. It wasn't until I discovered the work of Abraham Maslow that I understood my condition and could really come to terms with what I am, find some peace with it and resolve to do something about it which will satisfy me. People of this nature of self-actualizing are uncommon and difficult sometimes to detect if you don't know what you are looking for. I have friends with which I associate regularly but unfortunately they are mostly average and some are downright neurotic personalities and I really find it difficult to feel as though I am free to be just myself as natural as I can be and the whole situation is rather lacking of the type of stimulation I desire. I don't mean this to be a snobbish point of view just a simple matter of fact for which my friends and I have a good understanding. It is normal when I do open up to them that they are usually quite amused that they do not understand me very well. Sometimes they can become a bit irritated with me as they don't wish to participate in any intellectual endeavors, preferring to just get drunk. It's not that they are unintelligent it is just a matter of perspectives. I simply like to have these conversations and debates over intellectual subjects as it stimulates me and energizes me. Some of my friends on the other hand find it to be exhausting work.

Most average people generally have a limited view of themselves and the world around them and can be either quite impatient about forming an opinion to something and therefore cling to the first idea which seems to make sense to them or is generally accepted by most others with whom they associate or simply so disinterested in a matter they never put forth the energy to form an opinion as they see no point in doing so. A great many people simply go along with ideas of those they wish to associate with and don't bother form their own idea or to argue if they have a differing idea for fear of being exiled from the group. Most people never venture too far outside of the station they are born to. They are raised up and cultured to a limited view of the world around them and a limited understanding of reality as their views are often skewed by their own wishful thinking or anxieties or the ideas of the culture they are reared within or have affiliated themselves with. They are often indoctrinated to some form of optimism or pessimism which becomes the scope through which they view the world around them. This is where this book may serve as a tool for me to open a dialogue with like-minded individuals who have the same sort of difficulties as I do in acquiring stimulating and gratifying human interaction. To my perfectly normal average friends and even the neurotics: I do appreciate you and your companionship for what it is and I certainly don't mean you any insult; in fact I hope that you can find something for yourselves from the following work I lay out in this book. You my friends have been not only a source of information as I have studied you but also an inspiration to energize me in beginning this work to manifest my potential into reality.

The third intent is sort of matter of evangelical nature so to speak in that I am hopeful that my work may serve as a light to the average person to begin an understanding and appreciation for their individual identity. It is a beacon of hope and a challenge I offer to you to become all that you can be and to embrace everything your life has to offer. It is to say I hope you will get all you deserve because only those with the will to take action to attain something for themselves and accept all responsibility for it truly deserve a thing. So it is my hope and intent to inspire you to take command of your life as an individual, as it is my firm belief based upon the truth of creation that is the design and purpose of a life as God has intended from the beginning of creation.

I see people who struggle to understand themselves and their place in the world and how they should function in various circumstances; what they should do and what they should think of a situation they may be confronted with. They pose the questions, but usually end up clinging to some form of positivism or misguided interpretation of a theological perspective or twisted philosophical view which never really resolves their issue. They try to draw strength from an idea without any real knowledge or substance so inevitably it fails them. It is really a form of insanity in that one continues to repeat the same experiment or operate from the same misguided thought process in the hopes of attaining a different result than what they have already attained; the same result they have already determined to be insufficient. What I have to offer these people is a change in perspective; to open our minds to all true knowledge and understanding and take in to consideration the reality of life rather than living through our rose colored glasses view based upon our fears and anxieties and the wishful thinking. To ask the question and instead of accepting the first idea that comes along, we would seek to know and understand all possible perspectives of the thing and through comparison of those perspectives choose the answer that makes logical sense or at least the best and most efficient logic which can be found coupled with the idea of keeping an open mind which can always consider new information without prejudice or fear. They say the truth shall set you free, but most never really come to understand what true freedom is. True freedom is the loss of all constraint to the laws and ideology of mankind. It doesn't mean that you will go through life without regarding the laws and consequences of the society; it is an understanding of one's self to the notion that if the circumstances are right then it may become necessary to act in argument with the law or society's expectations for the realization of a greater good. I am confident that by our design if you can open your eyes to all possible perspectives for every possible circumstance or idea of what life can bring to you understanding that you can choose whatever action you see fit, you will choose to do the very right thing and the very good thing for which God would hope you would do; that is to say you would walk the path of God without pause or hesitation because for you it will have become a natural thing which requires little effort and causes you no fear or anxiety. You can be satisfied with putting forth your honest best effort to manage what is in your hands and let go of the portion of it which is not in your hands. You will serve your intended purpose to life just as God has designed you. We should all be free to share our lives, strengths and flaws unashamed and unafraid.

The ultimate overall intent of this work is the hope of presenting a message which creates a condition of restless thought within the reader for the idea of what one can do to make the world a better place for all mankind. I think it is a natural desire to want to create peace and harmony in the world one lives in, but the methods we utilize as a society are inefficient and ineffective to say the least as our view is skewed by the perspective of society and all too often by our own self-absorbed perspectives. That is to say that we are searching for the solutions to society's woes but we fail to understand that society is made up of individuals. We have been satisfied thus far in the pleasing of the majority as a means to determine how our society should function but when the individuals who make up the majority of society are in a state of dysfunction then the means we utilize to solve a problem of the majority creates more problems for the minority; this is injustice.

We seem in many ways to be a world lost in one form of mass hysteria after another. Each reason for one hysteria or another divides us all from one another. The world has become an angry and divided place. I wish to create my own form of mass hysteria I suppose but to a different end and by a different means. The means themselves are really ends as I will try to explain further on in this work of mine.

CULTURE DIFFUSION IN INTERNATIONAL HUMAN RIGHTS AND HUMAN RELATIONS

Concerns about individual human rights are as old as civilization. In the past 60 years concerns have been elevated to an international level in the fallout of World War 2 with the formation of the United Nations (UN) and the Universal Declaration of Human Rights of 1948. World powers have since seemingly utilized laws and treaties derived from the declaration to attempt to enforce the ideals of human rights through coercive means such as antiquated economic warfare strategies such as embargoes and sanctions. Revolutionaries of the 20th century such as Mahatma Gandhi and Martin Luther King Jr. have been the inspiration for passive means of overcoming human rights inequalities and the aid given to the United States during the American Revolution is probably the inspiration for our desires to help others in need throughout the world. The combination of these principles of inspiration has given birth to a new means of overcoming injustice in the world called Cross-Cultural or Trans-Cultural Diffusion.

The mechanism and concept of Cross-Cultural Diffusion is an ancient phenomenon and is a matter of study for cultural anthropologists and cultural geography and was first conceptualized by American anthropologist Alfred L. Kroeber in *Stimulus Diffusion* published in 1940. During his studies, Kroeber compared the historical patterns of how technology such as porcelain pottery, agriculture and weapons of warfare spread from one place to another and noted that when people are exposed to ideas or technologies they develop their own desires or need for them due to the advantages the materials offer and in turn adopt them as their own. Many of the examples of diffusion Kroeber cited in his paper can be attributed to commerce and simple interaction between different cultures, though most evidence of diffusion is indirect or inferred due to scant direct evidence, but according to Kroeber the conclusions of culture-diffusion are doubtless. Receiving cultures often expand upon fragments of systems taken from other cultures rather than adopting entire systems which make it difficult to pinpoint direct evidence of diffusion, but examination of historical records of cultures can infer the diffusion according to Kroeber. Though some instances of culture diffusion do occur as a result of conflict between cultures most occur simply through exposure through interaction.

Treaties concerning human rights are an attempt by those who have to persuade the "have not's". The treaties also serve to establish a rule of law to support the enforcement of the treaties through investigations, admonishment and ultimately economic reprimands, but these enforcement strategies do little or nothing to induce those responsible to act accordingly and create and undue hardship and suffering on the very people they are intended to protect. According to Roland Burke the first UN International Conference on Human Rights in 1968 established a needed focus on economic development and collective rights of the nation over individual rights based upon the idea that rights hold a priority behind basic human needs. You can't expect poor, uneducated and impoverished people to take much interest in civil and political rights.

Treaties which provide a source of reference to international law have little effect on changing the picture of human rights in the world. In their studies of human rights treaties and the nations which agree to them Emillie Hafner-Burton and Kiyoteru Tsutsui report that regimes which agree to these treaties are actually less likely to follow through on them and regimes who fear inciting opposition forces in their state are less likely to sign such treaties; they fear empowering people who are already bent on attaining rights. So basically, repressive regimes who have no one to oppose them in their state, are signing treaties as a means of gaining international legitimacy through symbolic commitment with no intent of abiding by these treaties at all and repressive regimes which fear being overthrown by opposition within their state simply won't sign any treaties, rendering such treaties moot.

No human being can begin to be concerned with something they have no knowledge of and knowledge is a product of education. Education is of little value to someone who is starving or breaking their back to feed and shelter themselves and their family. In his book *Motivation and Personality*, Abraham Maslow conceptualizes human needs and motivations into a pyramid of priorities divided into eight distinct levels categorized into three tiers called the *Hierarchy of Human Needs*. Maslow explains the first tier needs are basic physiological needs, the second are social needs and the third are esoteric/intrapersonal needs for self-actualization. We are all driven up this hierarchy by the fulfillment of those needs or much rather the security of those needs in their natural order of priority. It is logical to assume that what an individual needs a nation needs, as a nation or society is made up of individuals, therefore before a nation can concern itself with individual rights it must first secure the basic needs of the nation as a whole. Human Rights are social in nature as they establish rules and boundaries for human interaction, therefore the key to human rights is human interaction and thus the most effective strategy for the proliferation of human rights should be human interaction through the providence of basic human needs. Economic sanctions and embargoes create threats to the fulfillment of basic human needs and are therefore counter-productive to the proliferation of human rights.

Looking at the patterns of distribution within the UN Human Rights Council (UNCHR) we find nations divided into groups by geographic region and a member-state is elected by the geographic group to represent the geographic group. This is an interesting dynamic which has developed and is clearly a social strata based upon geography. In their studies of the significance of this regional dynamic within the UNCHR; *Sins of Commission? Understanding membership patterns on the United Nations Human Rights Commission,* Martin Edwards, Kevin Scott, Susan Allen and Kate Irvin find that member-states most likely to be elected to the council are dependent upon the human rights records of the region. Regions with overall poor records tend to elect the worst offender and regions with the better records elect the state with the best record. Furthermore in their study they show the significance of influence that states have upon their regional neighbors [Edwards]. Nations like individuals desire to find themselves in the company of likeminded personalities and so a need or desire to interact and influence your neighbor to secure your own needs is apparent. I supposed you could compare and contrast this to the difference between friends and family. States of a region are more like family than friends in that if you don't like the friends you have you can stop hanging out with them, but you're stuck with your family so you just have to make the best of them. Think of a boy who wants to be like his big brother and therefore follows the character development of the older boy.

In this new age of information and technology opportunities of diffusion abound. We can travel further and faster than ever before and sometimes without even leaving our home. Only regimes that prohibit or censor information technology and under-developed nations remain a challenge. However under-developed nations hold the advantage of being in need. Through international aid programs and international response to natural disasters we find opportunities to share culture. Ryan Goodman and Derek Jinks point to acculturation as a distinct process to influence state behavior and recommend reexamination of policy debates in international human rights and a framework to assess the costs and benefits of various design principles. Goodman and Jinks also point out several structural impediments to effective implementation of coercive and persuasive means of social influence. When a nation closes its doors and isolates itself from the international community such as Russia and China have in the past it presents a barrier to social influence. They simply tune it out and continue with business as usual. Goodman and Jinks call for a change in ideology in international policy with the idea that through commerce, open communication and mutual respect we can influence change through social means rather than anti-social means. Based upon the evidence an overhaul of the policies of enforcement of international law regarding human rights seems to be a logical step to take.

It seems only logical if the process utilized fails to yield the desired result, the data must be examined and evaluated to determine a change to the process which should steer the course to the desired achievement. The evidence from comparing studies of cultural development throughout the international community to study of personal human development more than clearly states relativity; eccentricities of nations/societies mirror those of individuals. World powers using warfare strategies in dealing with the enforcement are shooting themselves in the foot by creating conditions which counter the processes of development. I'm reminded of the warmonger notion of bombing a nation "back to the stone age". It is an inference which holds true that the impacts of warfare; whether physical or economic, imposes a state of regression. It is this regressive imposition which is the bullet in the foot of nation-states who chose war strategies as a means of foreign policy. Culture-diffusion has the potential to be our greatest weapon in the fight for liberty and rights and it is logical to think it is cheaper to build a nation than it is to destroy it and then rebuild it, so it is economical in terms of material capital as well as creates social capital through good will.

We must bear in mind that these management strategies of our society reflect our own personal strategies for dealing with our lives not only in social structures but within ourselves as well. Since it is logical to assume that what works within the individual and what works in society are of equal efficiency. So if these strategies are ineffective on a global scale we should expect them to be just as ineffective on an individual scale and everywhere in between. It would be better to calculate this perspective from the individual outward; that is to say that it is easier to see what works with an individual and what works for the individual can then be multiplied and supposed to a multitude. As it is with an individual it is also with a society; as a society grows, prospers and becomes secure in its needs it will quite naturally develop on its own a desire for human rights and the will to take action to attain those rights. Free will is the nature of the human being, so it is only natural that one will desire to be free of tyranny and oppression once they have secured their basic needs and their eyes have been opened to another way of life. They will on their own see the advantages of living in a free society and desire it for themselves and their families. Whether or not it will be necessary for these people to fight a bloody war for their independence is a matter of a case by case examination. We should help them if they ask for our help but in a limited capacity of providing aid only; it does us no good as a country to go around knocking off dictators, trying to install governments and actually creates more problems than it solves; as we are now finding from our actions in Iraq. Because we were so willing to go in and knock off a dictator in Iraq now we are faced with the need to do it to the next regime in Iran. It is the responsibility of the people of a nation to take their own action to develop on their own. No matter how good our intentions are, if the actions taken are not the design of the people then they will have no bond to what has been done. This is the same idea within the scope of dealing with personal social structures and intrapersonal issues. If someone is doing something which you wish they wouldn't do there is really no action you can take which will steer their course away from their behavior. There is no point in trying to punish them for their behavior in the hopes they will change and nothing you can offer them as a bribe will work either. Personal change, like social change is a slow process and takes real work. You can admonish the behavior and you can offer information; an idea to think about, which is like planting a seed, but only their interest will determine the effectiveness of this action.

The use of these warfare strategies is where I find great argument with some of my brethren of Christ. The strategies of evangelism are no different from domestic and international diplomacy. The church and therefore many Christians tend to favor the use of persuasive and coercive means of conversion rather than allowing their light to shine on its own. Religion or relationship with God is a personal individual endeavor first and foremost. I have seen recently in my experience of attending church a shift in this philosophy and policy in that I haven't seen the persuasive pitch to sell salvation to the listener or attempt to convince one of the dangers of the fiery death of eternal damnation if one doesn't convert. I like this change as it leaves only one strategy to work for the evangelical as the coercive and persuasive strategies are left unused.

NEUROTIC CULTURE

It is logical as I have stated to consider that what an individual needs a nation or society needs, the converse can be logical as well; that is to say that what a nation or society needs is what the majority of the society needs. So if we find our society in a condition of insecurity it is logical to assume that the majority of the individuals within that society feel insecure. If we find our society is suffering from a seemingly neurotic unhealthy mental state then it can be assumed this condition exists within the majority of the individuals within our society. It is no secret that our society has become consumed with image over substance ideology. It is a neurotic condition termed as narcissistic personality disorder. The narcissist is one who is insecure with who they are because they truly don't know who or what they are and where their own potentials lie or are uncomfortable with expressing it for fear of rejection from society. So instead of being who they are and becoming what they can be they put up a front; a fake persona of who they are. The problem is they lie to the world about who and what they are to save face and ignore their own weaknesses and shortcomings rather than face them and overcome them. This is the condition of our society ladies and gentlemen; this is what we have become. The problem or condition of the narcissist is really a sort of compulsive/obsessive disorder in which a person's personal growth and moral development has been stunted during childhood and they remain in an immature state where they cannot feel free and natural to be themselves. When they are confronted with a problem particularly a social challenge they react inappropriately and usually in a fashion of habit not so different from the OCD patient who latches the door in a certain order with the belief that doing so will yield a sort of mystical protection. It is not so different from the young child who is afraid of the darkness of his room and hides under the blankets believing that is the monsters don't see him then he is safe, while the reality would be if there were some monster in the dark set to destroy the child, the blankets would hardly offer any protection. The narcissist is obsessed with attention and any stifling of this attention produces a belief that they are under attack and their reactions are offensive and often outrageous and socially violent in nature in that they will attempt to attack their perceived aggressor in some manner socially. A good example would be when one perceives they will be rejected by someone else they will act out to force the issue thereby rejecting the other before they themselves are rejected. They will try to offend the person in a way which makes them uncomfortable so they might wish to leave. I can't help but see this same sort of attitude played out on television and in the streets by a whole generation of people obsessed with image. Anyone who doesn't take the tags and stickers off of their clothing items so it remains apparent to those around them what brand they are wearing is obviously stunted. There are a host of other social narcissistic characterizations to be found which the actors claim to be expressing their own individual style, but it is quite obvious if you are doing something that a multitude is doing in order to fit in then you aren't doing it for individual reasons of identity. When I walk into a place and three of the five people working there all have their ears gauged out to the size of a silver dollar which one is the one expressing their own individual style?

I find myself in the local bookstore looking for poetry to inspire my own. I find Whitman, Ginsburg, Poe Frost, Kilcher and then some others I am unfamiliar with and so goes my curiosity. I read this poem about this guy and his coffee, how much he drinks and how he supposes that his semen must taste of it because he drinks so much. I read another and yet another until I finally realize anyone that any idiot with a pen and the misfortune of being a coffee addict can get their poetry published. Those who dress to be fashionably out of style and wearing their supposed counter-culture like it were made by Gucci. The ego that compares itself to the outlaws of the sixties, protesting against inorganic coffee beans under black berets and scarves. Ideals used as punch lines to seek salvation for the sins of being born to the privilege of a home and parents who pay their way through life and college, providing them a car and a place to live away from home to solidify their false sense of independence they so passionately adore. White, upper, middle-class, white collar; the ultra-white wear only black. They sit around spouting high-minded ideals with big words; what can one hope to accomplish with poems about coffee and forging a false identity taken from false associations is something I fail to see. I don't see the being; the person, in their work. What little they do show of themselves is so shallow that bacteria would dehydrate in them if they were to become somehow infected. You can't express your depth if you never explore your depth and learn who you really are and practice being you own person. You can only express what you know of yourself to be and you can't begin to know yourself until you begin to study humanity to find your own humanity. You can't study humanity when you trap yourself in a pit of seeking acceptance by getting high on coffee and choking on cloves while turning your nose away from the shit that engulfs humanity. Humanity is lost away from the coffee house, hidden in alleyways and basements of abandoned buildings and dumpsters. The huddled masses shivering to stay warm, scavenging to survive and in the coffee cups of the working class in the early morning hours making their way to the factories still half asleep. It's found in the late nights while another third of them slave away only to get home with more work to do. The humanity of parents who have worked hard and sacrificed themselves on the altar of home and family to provide the life their children have taken for granted or spat on altogether. Time spent on homework, school plays, ball games and scouting goes unrewarded as their children struggle for identity and throw away the very thing which has shaped their lives; the love of those who love them most. It is sad to see these people live their lives so afraid of the good place they have come from. While they throw away a good life there are others who would give anything to have had the opportunity to have such a privileged rearing.

ABRAHAM MASLOW

For those of you not familiar with Maslow's Hierarchy of Human Needs I will begin with an explanation of the division of human needs and their significance to not only the human condition but also how they affect human behavior and how the drives to fulfill these needs define us each characteristically as either a human being or a human animal; there is a difference. Anyone who has had a basic psychology course has had some sort of introduction to the concept but in my experience it is hardly fitting the importance of his work. The hierarchy of human needs can be broken down into three tiers or levels. For the purpose of this discussion we will number them in the order of their respective priority to life.

1. The Physiological Needs: These needs are rather simple to understand they amount to the needs for air to breathe, water to drink, food to eat and then to more complex needs of shelter and of course the sexual drive which serves the purpose of procreation; though the product and ultimate purpose of the sex drive is social in nature it is nevertheless a physical compulsion.

2. The Social Needs: These needs are divided into two categories; one being personal social needs of personal safety and self-esteem and two being social esteem or belongingness and love and the respect of social safety. It is through social constructs we human beings have come from cave-dwelling nomadic scratching to

survive to possessing the power to share information at the speed of light around the world, leaving footprints upon the surface of the moon and of course the power to destroy ourselves and our world within minutes. These constructs are not the truth of that which makes the difference between human being and animal for even simple creatures such as ants construct physical social structures to support the social structure of their lives. Every creature that dwells within the earth, with the exception of some asexually reproductive microscopic organisms, has a drive to develop social structures.

3. The Need for Self-Actualization: This need is seemingly very complex and most of us never truly come to understand it or embrace it, yet it is the key difference between animals and human beings as it is the thing these other creatures lack. It is a drive to know and understand exactly what I am and what I am capable of and the search for a use of this potential. It is the realization of one's potential and the manifestation of this potential into external action upon the world. It can be confusing to understand it because it isn't a destination but rather a journey.

Self-actualization can be found through our roles, such as that of a parent, when one becomes what one can be as a mother or father or in a role of our career when one does the best that one can do. The greatest form of self-actualization can be exemplified by particular characters from history; world leaders as we refer to them. They are people who have stepped to the front of us and offered a point of view which leads and propel us in a direction towards a goal which is usually social in nature. These people stand apart from the masses and with great conviction spew fire from their mouths and seem to tap into some place in our hearts which stirs us to action. They are like the Greek god Prometheus who gives fire to mankind to light the darkness. These few of us who become everything one can be in a life and achieve great things for humanity such as the discovery of a cure for some disease, even a social disease such as racism or even something seemingly so small as simply serving to feed, clothe and house the underprivileged. Usually these people are stimulated to a fight with some great injustice of humanity. These are the shining examples of this condition called self-actualization; most self-actualizers can be found here and there and serve no great importance on the world stage perhaps but they are still doing their work in their own communities or travel far and wide to find a cause to support. Fame, fortune and great accolades are not the necessary hallmark of the self-actualized person. Many self-actualized people throughout history have suffered punishment and even death for their outcast views only to later be revered for their ideas. It is the desire to know and understand one's place in the world and what one might be able to do to make it a better place and taking the steps necessary to achieve this personal mandate or mission in life; sometimes the consequences of such action are drastic.

For some it is as simple as feeding the hungry or healing the sick or designing a better computer program or painting a masterpiece, but for others it is much like the opening narration given at the beginning of a Star Trek episode, it is the desire to explore the unknown and undiscovered to bring a light to the darkness of the world to expose the truth we so desperately need to set us free of the chains of ignorance and the oppression of enculturation. The most well-known self-actualized person is probably Jesus Christ. Whether you regard him as your lord and savior or as another prophet or a myth, he is the ideal example and accurate depiction of the character and motivation of the self-actualized person.

The ugly truth is that most of us never truly become all that we can be and most of us even fail to become the best we can be in our various roles in life as well. Most average people never truly try to become what they are because they have no idea of who they are and their potential because they never bother to ask the question of themselves. Some of us even falter into the belief that we have become all we can and become complacent, self-righteous, pompous hypocrites who fail to understand that self-actualization is a journey not a destination. Many of us just become disenchanted with the world and our place in it and simply give up doing any great good we might have imagined ourselves to do. We get caught up in the everyday life we lead and forget who we are and where we were going or even worse we lose hope for ourselves or hope in the belief that one person can make a difference. A friend of mine recently told me he doesn't vote because his vote doesn't count and that any hope of real change for the better in the politics of society in America is a lost cause because you can't get enough people involved. I had to point out to him that as long as people think like he does then he is right. No matter how big the challenge is it all starts with *you*. As it has been said the journey of a million miles begins with a single step so too the great challenge of social change must begin with the individual.

I won't be going into much depth and detail of the physiological needs because I think we all can grasp and understanding this concept quite readily. During the discussion of our other needs it is a good reference point from which to compare our drives to fulfill our other needs due to the fact that when one is confronted with a need it becomes their whole existence. It becomes the point of focus for their whole life and they find it difficult to think or act except to try to achieve the fulfillment of this need and their personal heaven can be nothing more to them but the place where this need is ultimately met. That is to say that any of these higher level needs can become as powerful to the individual as the need to breathe.

From here we can begin to put together and understand the social needs and their affects upon human existence both good and bad. So we should start at the beginning and try to put the pieces together in a logical manner to understand how the social our social drives have benefitted us as individuals and as a species and also caused our faults and hold our potential downfall.

SELF-ACTUALIZATION OF THE CAVEMAN

Here we are on the plains of Africa searching for food. By ourselves we would hunt for hours for a meal and spend a great portion of our time preparing our equipment for hunting or finding shelter, all the while our heads on a swivel to save us from the dangers such as predators which would make a meal of us. We are busy people by ourselves with not much time for idle and nonproductive thoughts and hands. In a group however we have great advantages as we can specialize our roles to get the work done faster and more efficiently and help to protect one another in the process. Because of this we find that we have some extra time for exploring our thoughts which we may utilize to paint on cave walls or tell stories or invent some new and better way to find and kill our food which in turn gives us more and more free time to think and invent. In my opinion as it is now (I say it this way because my opinion could always change), it had to be someone who had this extra time to play with plants to figure out that they could be cultivated which is the big leap towards modern civilization. It was the formation of society which made civilization possible. It was people gathering together for common good and focusing on what could be done to make life better for each and all of us.

Social construct is unfortunately the cause of social difference and ultimately prejudice. One person's idea is liked by others and through this process of assimilation we have culture and ethnicity which can be good things and even though it is perfectly alright when another group has a different idea it is when the dislike of this idea by another group leads them to make ignorant associations and generalizations about the other group; "I don't like their ideas and no wonder; the cause of their ill idea is the color of their skin or the shape of their eyes.". It usually begins whether good or bad with one person who seems to have a greater insight than the rest of the group. The group follows along with them, failing to find their own truth to the matter and now we have bigotry.

A good example from social experience is the group characteristic to follow the leader. Johnny is being a jerk to someone and even though his friends may not really approve of what he is doing, because each person fears being outcast and ridiculed by the group each one goes along with the behavior and reinforces it sometimes by the simple act of not doing anything at all. It is same scenario regardless of what type of group it may be whether it is in a bar or in a church. One person has an idea and the others adopt the idea because they lack the strength of individual character to resist or they simply don't have a better idea themselves because they never explored the matter of subject for themselves, instead choosing to simply follow along blindly. The preacher says the Bible is the whole truth and nothing but the truth and it is to be believed above any and all other notions of reason and logic and because he is regarded in such high esteem by the group. The group members really haven't examined and taken in for themselves their own truth and their own individual walk with faith and the fact they are coerced under threat of eternal damnation if they don't accept this belief simply adopt this idea as their own without any effort and go right ahead and pass it on to the next person as it has been put to them with no logical or reasonable idea to support their claim.

Socialization is a balancing act if one is to maintain their individuality. As Carl Jung has pointed out to us, becoming overly socialized to a culture whether in the form of a society, a government or a religious mass is the stumbling block which obliterates the individual. Handing over responsibility for our lives and the condition of our existence to the government we become statistical units because we expect government to treat us all equally the same for good or bad and we rely upon them for their good grace and protection from all that may harm us. Handing over responsibility for our spiritual life and condition to a mass or even another person has a similar consequence and further more is the loss of the ultimate truth of creation; we are designed to be individuals. Blindly following along with the doctrine of the church without question we only trade one form of slavery for another and the thing which we have determined will protect us from all evil becomes the namesake for our sacrifice as we are threatened to our very souls to go along with the group or perish. Unfortunately it is usually the few who understand how to manipulate the system to their advantage who prosper at the expense of the meek.

WALKING THE PATH OF GOD

Some of you may misunderstand me and may accuse me of being of no faith, but the truth couldn't be further. Religion, or if you prefer as I do, a relationship with God, is not contrary to individuality or self. Did God set your alarm clock to tell you what time you needed to get up? Did God hit the snooze button to allow you nine more minutes of sleep? Self-will and ego are not the same. Self-will is the potential drive to action and ego is pure selfish nature driven by instincts of survival. When self-will and God's will are one in the same, we act in a Godlike manner naturally without thought or hesitation as it is not difficult to do so and we receive much joy in it and it becomes self-pleasure not self-sacrificing. It is the ego we must overcome and crucify. It is referred to as flesh in church but I think this is a confusing way to explain it; it is the animal side of us not the matter of which we are made. It isn't about destruction of the animal side of us but rather mastering the animal side. Just as it is said the love of money is the root of all evil; it's not that money is evil as money is an only an idea and fabrication of mankind and has no personality, but the love and reverence of it can drive a person to act in manners which have evil nature or consequence. It is a good servant, but a poor master. As with any great enemy we must know them to conquer them. We all have within us the seeds of great good and terrible evil. It is a necessity for the purpose of free will that we have them both in great and equal quantity. One is capable of as much good as they are evil. Many of us choose to try to hide or ignore the dark side of us because we are afraid of it because we don't understand it. We fail to realize the less we know about a thing the more power and awe it has over us. Imagine how frightened people of the middle ages would be if they were confronted with something as harmless as a cell phone. They would think it were some kind of mystical thing to be feared or revered as a thing of God. This is the way many of us see the evil in us. We want to hide it away from ourselves and everyone around us for fear of being an outcast. We are taught to lead our spiritual lives as something separate from our minds and bodies. If all things in creation exalt God then why should our minds and bodies be any different? It is the unifying of all that we are, through discovery of ourselves, by the examination of all possible perspectives of what we have the potential to become which lights the path of God. The realization of our potential and the manifestation of it from within upon the world is to walk in this path. It is as if I am no longer stumbling around trying to follow God, but instead I walk beside him quite well as he intended me to because I understand and know where he is going. An analogy I like is to compare life to a hand of poker. Most of us hobble along with the hand we have been dealt without knowing the rules; realizing the truth of the game which is that we can create our own Aces and change our own hand. Nobody would bet their life; their soul on a hand without doing just that if they realized they could.

SOBERING THOUGHTS

I am reminded of my Dad and his sobriety. For the first seventeen years of my life he was a drunk. He was angry at most everything and everyone in the world and quite often very aggressive and sometimes violent towards his family. He has been sober for eighteen years now, but more importantly his attitude and outlook on life has changed allot. Through Alcoholics Anonymous and The Twelve Step Program he has had successful recovery so far. I say "so far" because recovery is considered a never-ending process to my Dad and others like him. They recognize the need to ever vigilant to the reality of the fact that anyone can slip at any time and derail. So the recovering alcoholic never asserts himself to the belief that he is cured of his disease and as a result forces himself to maintain his work. The first step towards sobriety is the recognition of the condition of being an alcoholic. No one else, it is said, can determine for you if you are an alcoholic, it is something you must determine for yourself. Any layman can look at someone's behavior and probably make a precise diagnosis of alcoholism, but what it really means though is that sobriety if it is to be successful has to be based upon an honest desire to change after the individual has honestly recognized they have a problem. Alcoholism isn't about alcohol. The abuse of alcohol or drugs is only a symptom of a personality defect. This is the issue which must be recognized by the alcoholic if they are to have any hope of recovery. You can't fix something if you don't think anything is wrong with it or don't understand what the problem is and nobody can fix you but yourself and God. God through his gift of free will has given you the option if you so desire to choose to not allow his help. That is a powerful statement and I'm sure it may ruffle some feathers, but the point is clear so I will state it again and more certainly: Not even God can change you if you don't want to be changed! It is the only logical conclusion if the doctrine of free will is to be believed. To satisfy those of you who would say this is disrespectful of God I will put it this way; God created us to be individuals and to choose our own path in life and he will not interfere to do so would be contrary to the purpose of creation. The point of all of this is that unless you can take an honest accounting of all that you are, your weaknesses will continue to dominate your life and you will be doomed to repeat the same cycles of self-destructive behavior. I think it was Ben Franklin who said insanity is repeating the same actions and expecting a different result.

To conquer the evil in your heart you must recognize it before you can overcome it. Going to church every Sunday all your life is of no consequence; it doesn't make you perfectly good and well. Listening or reading and regurgitating bible verse or sermon doesn't make you right. The idea that a string of words in a certain order gives them some sort of mystical, magical power over evil is ludicrous and elevates the bible to a status of an idol. It is this idolatry and superstition which is your stumbling block. Throwing your hand about your body in a cross-like configuration, possessing a crucifix and chanting bible verse will not protect you from any evil at all; least of all the evil in your own heart. As I am writing this book there is a pastor of one of the largest congregations in the country who has been prolific in the persecution of homosexuals has been accused of having inappropriate relations with two young men. The responses from those who obviously follow his teachings have shown that they refuse to believe such a thing and there is no way he could ever have done such a thing. He is another human being and is quite capable of being wrong and doing the wrong thing so it is entirely possible and since his accusers are putting themselves at such great risk by coming out and filing a suit against him I would say it is quite probable. I'm not assigning guilt or judging him, I am simply stating the fact that he is just as fallible as anyone and greater men have made bigger mistakes. It could be a matter of a misunderstanding; the evidence will tell the story, so I will leave it at that.

I have never found anywhere in my life a greater concentration of self-righteous hypocrisy, ignorance and arrogance as I have in church, with one exception; the Congress of the United States as seen on C-Span. The foundation of individual free will (whether or not you believe it to be a matter of faith or not) as John Locke put it, is what makes each of us the ordained ruler of our own kingdom of individuality. It is for the protection of our natural rights that we enter into covenant/agreement with society. The church is an external social construct; it is an entity or device which is designed to serve our social needs for belongingness, acceptance and love. The church you attend was built by the hands of men and is managed by the minds of men therefore perfectly capable of being just as flawed as man. The bible cannot be 100% accurate and reliable as has been suggested to me in church, as it is a product of the hands of men and as such is just as potentially hazardous and faulty as man and anything else which man has made. When I receive a book which is written by no other hand but God himself and am told by God himself that it contains all truth then I will accept it as perfect and complete. I have been given free will and a mandate from my God to choose my life. I am not subject to your judgment; you have no authority over me. If I choose for my life something which is displeasing to God he will deal with me in my time. I understand and accept that I am flawed. I am no better or worse than anyone else who lives or has ever lived in this world. What I am, is not what matters, it is what I do which makes the difference, but it is my desire to do what I am or to be what I do. That is to say that what I am should be what I am not only in nature but in demeanor as well. That what I am is characterized in what I do as what I truly am is manifest into the real world.

We must address the issue of persecution of homosexuals by the Christian Church. It is not the place of any of us to cast judgment upon another for the life they live which has no effect upon us. I am of no opinion nor do I care to form or offer an opinion of the homosexual condition as to whether it is a choice of lifestyle or a biological imperative; it is of no concern or authority of mine to judge them or attempt to place limits upon their lives. Marriage isn't a Christian invention and is therefore not exclusive and it is no ill affect to any heterosexual marriage for homosexuals to get married. Marriage and its purpose and value are a matter for the married couple to determine for themselves and no other person should have or attempt to have authority over it. There is nothing from God or any other source which compels me to believe that I should persecute them or that I have the right and purpose to persecute homosexuals regardless of whether I disagree with it or believe it to be a sin. Mind your own business with your own marriage; get the plank out of your own eye and don't worry about the splinter in someone else's.

SAFETY NEEDS

The safety needs are the primary reasons for the formation of society and therefore the foundation of social needs. It is for the security of our physiological needs that we enter into agreement with others to form society. When these needs for safety are threatened we are quite naturally driven to respond. Maslow noted that in infants this threat danger reaction is so clear because children at this age haven't been en-cultured to inhibit their reaction, whereas adults have been taught to inhibit their reaction at all costs, so even when an adult's safety is threatened we may not see it on the surface. You can see it however in some, especially in emotional reactions to stimulus such as is the case of interpersonal relationships when a partner acts out in anger or frustration or in another obsessive manner such as stalking. They are driven by their fear of rejection and feel a real threat to their personal existence primarily because they fail to satisfy their own needs, instead choosing an external source of personal comfort in this case another person. It could very well be said that it is childlike behavior and is evidence of a lack of personal maturity.

The safety needs for most people have to do with justice, fairness and consistency in relationship with society as a whole and on a more personal level within the family. Injustice, unfairness and inconsistency in parents seem to make a child feel anxious and unsafe according to Maslow. He goes on to point out the central role of the parents and normal family setup is indisputable. Quarreling, physical assault, separation, divorce or death within the family may be particularly terrifying and parental outbursts or rage, threats of punishment, name calling, harsh language, rough handling and physical punishment sometimes illicit such total panic and terror in children we must assume more is involved than the physical pain alone. The average child prefers safety, predictability and organization in their world. Children who are reared in a peaceful and loving family tend to react to dangers in much the same reasonable manners as adults; they tend to perceive the world more clearly and realistically.

Here is another argument I have with my brethren of the church. You say spare not the rod, lest you spoil the child. I tell you that when you use physical punishment as a means of discipline you teach your child that it is perfectly acceptable to hit someone else when they do something you perceive to be wrong because that is exactly what you are doing. From the time a child is capable of understanding language your focus shouldn't be on punishment but instead upon education. If you can help your child to understand why they did what they did and what is wrong with the thought process that led them to their mistake you will save them from making many more mistakes which would have been based upon that same sort of thought or logic. This, in and of itself along with your disapproval of their action is good enough for them to form their own guide to do the right thing. On the other hand the more you oppress someone the more they will rebel against you. The more someone is exposed to something the more immune they become to its affects; meaning that the spankings or beatings become tolerable. The person will simply weigh the decision to do something wrong based upon whether or not they can tolerate the potential punishment and they will go ahead and do as they wish as they realize they have been hit before and it really wasn't so bad. It is a natural thing for the individual to desire their own will; it is how we are naturally designed. Free will is what drives us as individuals to be what we are or what we think we ought to be. The more you oppress someone the more fiercely they will rebel it is a natural response. This is what we see in homes where parenting is sort of totalitarian dictatorship; the example of the preacher's daughter being the wild one.

Dillen Steeby

The average mentally healthy adult in society is fairly satisfied with his safety needs. Society is for the most part peaceful and dangers are few and far between. However the economically and socially downtrodden are of the greatest opportunity for improvement. It is, in my mind, tragic that in this day and age with the state of our technology that there are still people in the world who are starving and threatened by violence and tyranny. Until every being upon this world is free then none of us are truly free. I mean freedom in every sense of the word. Some of us have taken up cause to expand the rights of others in other places, but you can't expect people who are impoverished and poor to have much to do about their rights. As I have mentioned before there are three strategies for trying to bring change to another person and only one really works. You can coerce them, you can persuade/bribe them or you can expose them to your idea through your actions and allow them to take it up for themselves on their own. I can beat you to your death, but I cannot change what is in your heart. You can say you agree with me to get me to stop, but I have accomplished nothing. I can bribe you into my idea and you could accept my offer only to shut me up and I haven't accomplished anything. I can extend my hand in brotherhood and offer my assistance and friendship to you expecting nothing from you and if I am proven true you will admire me for my grace and take up my cause as your own because I have infected you with love and you will be compelled to repeat my performance. What a beautiful place the world would be if we were all consumed with helping one another instead of focusing on the differences between us.

ESTEEM, BELONGINGNESS AND LOVE

Everyone needs a stable and high evaluation of themselves. Self-respect and self-esteem come from self. Satisfaction of this condition brings feelings of strength, confidence, and personal value of being useful to the world. Lacking the ability to fulfill these needs leads to feelings of inferiority, weakness and helplessness and may lead one to seek these needs through external sources, possibly to a neurotic extent as is the case with the narcissist. If you seek your self-esteem needs through external sources you have no alternative but to be fake because if you were to satisfy these needs through your own mechanisms you would feel no shame of who or what you are. If you don't like something about yourself then work on it to change it honestly. I promise you that if you work at it and keep it up you can do it in very little time. Sure it's tough to get started and you will be tempted from time to time to revert back to old habits, but with practice you will get good at it and it will pay off. When you start getting the results you want then it will be easy to make it natural habit. If you have a bad temper, then come up with some sort of system or strategy to manage it and just like anything else, with practice and time you will sort it out. This living a lie to the world is what we see in the narcissistic personality disorder and though it is an extreme example it serves to highlight the same operating procedures of many people who wouldn't necessarily be classified as neurotic, but rather misguided. This person is afraid to be honest with others about who they are so they put on a persona;

most of us do wear some sort of persona in our daily lives but the NPD takes this to the extreme. Their self-esteem and opinion of themselves is so horribly low that they need constant attention and reassurance from others. They want people to think they are beautiful inside and out and need acknowledgement of this through constant attention. If they feel the attention or respect they need is threatened they often will attempt to attack someone else in a social structure such as targeting someone they perceive as weak within a group of people. They choose only those that they know they can attack without much recourse, as bullies usually do. The narcissist is quite calculating in manipulating others but isn't much of a stretch from the manner in which the average non-neurotic person operates.

Before you can tackle your needs of belongingness and really feel a connection to another human being you need to be comfortable with who you are and what you are doing with your life so that you can be who you really naturally are, otherwise you're simply faking who you are and your relationship is just as fake as you are. Your relationships with others can only be as fulfilling and honest as you are with them and you can't be honest with others until you are honest with yourself. Relationships are characterized by honesty, trust and communication. Every relationship regardless of how deep or effective it is has these three qualities it is just the quantity or quality of these characteristics which makes the difference in how stimulating the relationship is to you. If you say you don't trust someone at all then there is still a measure of trust in the relationship it is simply a mathematically negative value. The same is true of honesty and trust. Everything is measurable; it is simply a matter of finding or designing a standard of comparison.

When your self-esteem is based upon true deserved respect for yourself then you should have no lack of confidence in facing the world and receiving the same level of respect and esteem from others. Become what you are. That is to say become the person inside you desire to be on the outside. Make your ideal of who you would like to be a true reality. In other words, walk the walk. Become the genuinely courageous, just and honest person you admire from the inside. Realize your potential and manifest it into the real. Don't place style over substance.

THE HUMAN ANIMAL VS. THE HUMAN BEING

The two basic divisions of the hierarchy of needs we have classified as physiological and social are the same basic needs of every animal on the planet. Though many of those animals' social relationships and eccentricities may not be as complex as ours they are none the less the same basic program parameters. It is as simple as the program which operates the computer upon which I am processing this page. It is all zeroes and ones. It is a matter of a condition being met or not being met to illicit a response to either fulfill the condition or if the condition is met then move to the next order of operation. That isn't to say that if you get hungry all of the sudden you don't care about your friends and loved ones. It is a matter of threat analysis. If the condition is being threatened then you will act in some way to secure the fulfillment of the condition. The point is that every animal on the planet has these same drives and works in pretty much the same way. So operating our lives at these basic levels we are truly no more than animals. If we do nothing more with ourselves we still have untapped potential which waits to be realized and manifest. So when we feel secure in these needs and desires or at least we don't fear whether or not the condition is being met we feel good about ourselves and we will find an urge to do something powerful. We will find ourselves a new thing to consume or energies as we seek to realize our greatest personal potential and find some way to express it or make something good and special of it. This is self-actualization.

A poet must write, a musician must play and compose, a painter must paint if they are to be at peace with themselves.

When we come to self-actualization we become consumed with a desire to know and understand the things we see as strange and mysterious. We have overcome our fears of the unknown and with great energy we set the natural world in which we live into a framework and study these mysteries and how they fit into the scheme of things. We imagine ourselves as spectators of the play of life. Unfortunately it is also found that intelligent people leading monotonous and unchallenging lives will fall into a stupor as they lose their zest for life and eventually become as dull and uninteresting as the life they lead. Intellect and motivation as it seems are like muscles which need to be exercised to improve their strength and stamina. Live like the alcoholics; one day at a time and sometimes one moment at a time. Embrace your life from day to day never taking it for granted and keep your wits about you being ever vigilant in finding the little things that make life beautiful; in short, truly live every minute of your life you possibly can.

The point is that any animal has drives to satisfy physiological needs and social needs so if our lives never lead us to anything beyond these motivations we aren't being human at all we are simply another primate and are no more human than an animal at the zoo. Any wild dog will risk its neck to save or defend a pack mate, so it's not enough to say you would risk your life for someone else in danger as a measure of a human being. Being human is something different entirely. It is the realization of the truth of our animal drives and the ability to step outside ourselves and understand the world from a perspective which may not be our own. How else can we get past the things which are different about us and work on the things we have in common? Through understanding and practice we can work to overcome or master the animal drives in us and become something more than a human animal. When we define ourselves and the role we wish to play in life as being some great mission and take on the challenges to fulfill this role is when we begin to   human.

I have always had a desire to write and to be a published author for as long as I can remember. I always thought it would be in poetry but I never really came to grips with it until now. I've written countless poems and even shared quite a few of them with people over the years but I never really felt right about what I wanted to say until now. I have a deep and powerful drive to reach out to people of all walks of life, all stripes and all classes for the purpose of making a difference to make the world a better place for all of us. I am certain this desire is derived from my belief and admiration of a loving God, the teachings of Jesus Christ and my wish to become as much like them as is humanly possible in this life. I can't help but feel myself compelled to a great mission to set a cornerstone for the foundation of a new world of peace. My wish ultimately is to destroy everything which destroys us; this is my mission and my mandate in life. I wish to become a powerful voice in this world. I know from experience in dealing with people that I am good at tapping into others potential or at least seeing the potential in others they may not see in themselves. I can get someone motivated to do whatever it is they are doing on a higher level. I can stimulate the higher functions of the human being in others. It is my firm belief that if I can motivate just one person at a time then it simply becomes a matter of math in that if I write this book and get it into your hands I'm spreading my disease so to speak. I wish to infect your mind with thoughts and ideas that I know are already there anyway. I hope after reading this book you find yourself consumed with desire to discover yourself and define your mission in life and the person you always wanted will become the person you are.

If I am successful you will tell someone about this book and they may read it and when this book has been read by ten million people or maybe more I will have made a pretty good dent in the way things are. My purpose is driven by the belief that the kingdom of heaven isn't some city which will fall from the sky, but is something which needs to come from within each of us. It is the realization of the potential of what the world could and should be and the manifestation of it upon the world. When every person on this planet is truly free and no longer seeks to divide and conquer instead seeking to embrace and truly love others as themselves we will no longer need the guns and the bombs. Regardless of my theological perspective; that is to say that even if I didn't believe in God, I know that the way things are should be different and can be. So I refuse to accept the way things are and demand that they be different while at the same time understanding that change is slow and it all begins with one; myself.

SELF-ACTUALIZING PEOPLE; HUMANS BEING

These people seem to be fulfilling themselves and doing the best they are capable of doing and becoming what they are. No one is perfect but you could say that if you are being the best you can be then what more can you ask of yourself. Many of us fail to realize our potential and therefore may think we are the best we can be and fail to act to become any better than what we are. So how do you measure it? How do I know if I'm a person in this condition? The following are some noted characteristics from Maslow's studies of self-actualizing people.

Self-actualizing people tend to have a more efficient perception of reality and more readily discern the fake and dishonesty in personality and more efficiently judge people and situations in matters of the arts, music, science, politics. They are good at predicting the future in relations to whatever facts may be at hand at the time because these predictions are based upon facts of reality rather than wish, desire, anxiety or any generalized character state of optimism of pessimism. These predictions are also improved by the ability to see all possible perspective outcomes of a given circumstance. This superior ability of perception gives one the power to reason logically and come to conclusions efficiently. They aren't bogged down in their thoughts by manmade concepts, expectations, beliefs and stereotypes which most people confuse with the real world. They don't fear the unknown as most people but rather like to discover strange or unknown things and can find the beauty in them. It can be characterized as intellectual power but having a high IQ is really no yardstick as many people of high IQ can suffer the same misdirections as the average person; they can and do often fail to act upon their intellectual energies out of fear or laziness.

Self-actualizing people don't worry about the ghosts in the closet or feel nervous walking by the cemetery at night or have any other desire to protect themselves from imaginary or superstitious dangers. They don't suffer from crippling guilt or shame or extreme anxieties over past experiences as they quite readily come to terms with the mistakes they have made and move on. It isn't to say they don't care about the mistakes they make or don't feel guilty or ashamed of things they have done, it is simply they don't agonize over or ignore it; they simply evaluate it and move on with what they have learned from it. They have come to terms with themselves and their own faults as well as the faults of others and accept things as they are with the understanding that you cannot change what is done and you cannot change someone else who doesn't want to change. Observing what is, without argument or demanding that it be otherwise as to do so is a waste of time and energy; it is inefficient. This may cause you to think I'm contradicting my previous statement where I stated that I do not accept the way things are and demand they be changed. In this instance I am speaking of other individuals on a personal level.

Let me cite an example. I have a friend who suffers from a narcissistic condition. I know I cannot change him if he doesn't want to change and trust me he doesn't want to change. However I am no less his friend over it and I don't stress or agonize about his neurotic behaviors nor do I accept them. When he gets to acting up I don't hesitate to admonish his behavior, but I do so with the understanding that he probably won't change so I have no expectation of his behavior changing. If however I accept his behavior without giving him some admonishment at all and no one else gives him reprimand for his behavior then he will never see any advantage to changing his behavior and thus I his friend doom him to certain hopelessness. It is with hope for him that perhaps he will grow a little bit someday that I bother. If I didn't care for him I'd simply not associate with him at all. I don't berate him or ride his case about any of it I simply challenge his lapse of reason by offering reason and leave it at that. It is usually only the times when he is doing or saying something I see as some sort of injustice towards another person or group of people when I decide to say something. Most of the time it is just a matter of asking a question which challenges the validity of the thought which drives his behavior. We all take heed of the social environment we find ourselves in and try to refrain from behavior which may embarrass or irritate those we associate with. Sometimes though we slip and let something slide we shouldn't have and need a little nudge to put us back on track.

As far as the world is concerned I think it is a similar scenario to say that I don't agonize over the state of things and certainly don't expect great change to happen quickly. Social change is a slow process after all. At the same time if myself plus no one else take no action at all then it is certain things will never change and if I didn't care I wouldn't bother to try.

Self-actualizing people tend to eat and sleep well even during life circumstances where the average person and certainly the neurotic person may be unable to eat or sleep at all. They have a strong distaste however for the artificial characteristics of the average person such as guile, hypocrisy, lying/dishonesty or trying to impress others; these artificialities are absent in the self-actualizing person to an unusual degree. They simply have no interest in wasting time and energy being dishonest about who they are or what they observe. Of all the lies I ever told the worst were the ones I told myself; being dishonest with others is one bad thing but to be dishonest with yourself is the worst. Self-actualizing people are so comfortable with their own shortcomings they don't feel a need to hide or be fake about who or what they are. They say what they think whenever they feel like saying it and do what they think they should just as they think they should without unnecessary worry about what others might think. That is not to say they don't feel bad about some things because as anyone does they too make mistakes. The things that bother the self-actualizing person the most have to do with their own character weaknesses/improvable shortcomings, personal bad habits or shortcomings of the culture or group with which they associate or identify. The best way to deal with mistakes you have made is to step outside the situation so you can remove the emotional clutter and view it objectively. Pretend the same scenario exists but with different participants; see from a bystander's perspective.

Self-actualizing people are spontaneous of thought and actions in an unusually unconventional way and quite naturally, as if with no effort at all. In fact conventionality is something this person wears much like a shirt in order to blend in with a society which cannot truly understand them. They don't wish to offend hurt or fight with anyone over trivial matters so they will go through the rituals of convention with a smile and grace that is pleasing to others, but this cloak is easily cast aside at moments when this person is stimulated to arousal; it never keeps them from doing anything important. Most importantly to this person it is when they are in the company of individuals who do not expect routine behavior this burden may be relinquished for a time and allow the self-actualizing person to be more natural and free.

Self-actualizing people live by their own code of rules and ethics which are not constrained by the rules of society yet they are the most ethical people as the ordinary ethical behavior of most people is manifest out of convention to society rather than by personal preference and so the average person is usually only as honest as society requires them to be. The self-actualizing person will operate by the same code regardless of whether anyone is available to judge their behavior or not. Because of this alienation from the ordinarily accepted hypocrisies and inconsistencies of social life these people often feel like aliens from another world; they just don't feel like they fit in. They usually behave in conventional ways because nothing of importance is at stake and they know that people will be hurt or embarrassed by any other behavior.

The differences in the life of the self-actualizing person and the average healthy person are in quality as well as quantity. They are not striving as people strive but developing and attempting to grow to perfection in their own style. That is to say that most average people are stimulated to action to fulfill some deficiency in their life, but the Self-actualizing person feels no deficiency for these normal social needs like the average person does and instead act out of a desire to fulfill something that isn't necessary for normal life really but to them seems to be a necessity of their life. It is the same overwhelming drive that a hungry person will feel for a meal but the purpose and goal isn't something of necessity as the normal person would need. Most people strive to attain what they lack, but self-actualizing people are not trying to achieve what they lack but rather to reach for something based upon an impulse which isn't based upon the lack of something. They are focused upon problems outside their own needs and desires, but for their own motivations and tend to be problem centered rather than ego centered. They have a mission which is a broader purpose and horizon, a vision of what can be and they carry themselves with a sense of serenity and lack of anxiety for the immediate concerns of life.

Self-actualizing people tend to be less needing of human interaction. They can be quite comfortable by themselves and tend to like solitude to a greater degree than the average person. They can't be defined as introverted at all though, they are simply detached and it is this detachment which serves to keep them calmly above the battle and undisturbed by circumstances which would produce turmoil in the average person. They can deal with personal misfortunes and handle negative circumstances quite calmly remain objective even in the face of great personal tragedy of indignity. It is this objectivity, this way of looking at one's self from an outside perspective and be more problem centered than ego centered. They tend to have the ability to concentrate to an unusual degree which may produce absent-mindedness of their surroundings which is why they can sleep, eat, laugh and smile even in times of great strife. This detachment isn't without consequence though as most average people may view the self-actualizing person as being cold, snobbish, unloving and even hostile due to the fact that the average relationship is more needing of warmth, support and exclusiveness. Self-actualizing people simply do not need of others in an ordinary sense. I'm reminded of *Star Wars: Revenge of the Sith*, when Yoda tells Skywalker that he must train himself to let go of everything he fears to lose because it is his attachment, his possessive attitude and desire to control something he doesn't have the power to control which leads to his downfall.

I have some friends with which I associate, but I don't spend as much time on them as they spend on each other in the group. I don't feel the need to. I'm comfortable by myself and even my own family is a sort of detached relationship. I do from time to time wish that I could spend more time with them but that is simply my life as I see it and there is only so much time in a day and only so many days in a life so it is a matter of time affordability. I love my son more than anything in the world and if I lost him I would of course be devastated as any parent would be, but I would be able to accept it and move on.

My Mom was a wonderful woman and I love her dearly and yes I miss her since she has passed away three years ago from cancer, however on the day she died I didn't feel the need to be there to her last breath and some of my family have taken the view of me as being cold-hearted about the matter because I left and went to see a guy about a garden tiller I wanted to buy from him. Some of my family members judged me very harshly over this, but I didn't need to be there because I already had all the time I needed to be at peace and I accepted the fact that she was going to die soon. I called family to give them the opportunity to be with her in her last hours and called a priest to administer her last rights out of respect for her catholic traditions. When they arrived I left. On my way I called my Aunt Mary to see if she wanted me to put Mom on ice before having the funeral so that she and Larry could come up from Texas to be here; she said she was fine with it as she and Larry had been up to visit just a month prior and that anything she had needed to give or receive with Mom was satisfied, and then I called the funeral home to make the arrangements. I tended to my Mom as her power of attorney and took care of her while she was dying. I chased after the pills, the doctor appointments, chemotherapy and served as her nurse and maid watching this horrible disease destroy the woman I loved and admired the most; the one person in the world who would throw herself under a bus for me. I had seen enough and had done all I could do for her and there was nothing to be lost by not being there watching her unresponsive body exhale its last breath. I do miss my Mom every day and I'm fairly certain I will never have a more loyal and loving friend as she was to me. It is this detachment which may seem to many people to be ruthless as in the case when I find a friend to be dishonest with me I can walk away from that friendship and not give it a second thought. It's not that I'm cold and ruthless it is simply my understanding of the nature of relationships. Many people want to try to put relationships into some sort of category that doesn't require that either person in the relationship to be wanting or needing of the other but the simple truth of relationships is they are all about exchange of something. There are costs and benefits to every relationship and if the exchange is costing you too much and not paying you enough to be balanced then it is leaving you deficient and if you don't eliminate the deficiency it is a point of insanity. If you can come up with a strategy to repair the relationship or at least manage it successfully then by all means do so, but if it is destructive then you have to let it go and move on without hesitation or regret.

The point is that most average people are motivated by deficiencies; lack of something they need or desire. The self-actualizing person is comfortable or satisfied with their needs and desires so that they are now motivated by growth and are not dependent upon the people, culture or the world. They are dependent on their own growth and development and realizing their potential. Being independent of their environment gives them stability in the face of the trials and tribulations of life, so they can remain quite serene in circumstances which would drive the average person to suicide. Deficiency motivated people must have someone else to lean on to satisfy their needs for love, safety, respect, etc. So it is to say that the self-actualizing person is reliant upon themselves for needs which are beyond the normal animal drives of the physiological and social needs.

According to Maslow's studies the only way to come to this point of independence of love and respect is to have been given plenty of this love and respect in the past; which is why I choose to regard my son not as MINE but rather as another individual with a life of his own to live. I am his parent not his owner or oppressor. I believe that even though the circumstances of my youth in growing up in an alcoholic and codependent home somewhere I figured out that as insane as it may have seemed my father was as he was because it was all he could understand as the best he could do for me because he did love me. I always knew my Mom loved me and she only wanted me to be happy in life; she was always overt about this. My Dad was hard on his kids because he wanted us to be strong for a day when he wouldn't be around to protect us from the ugly side of life and he didn't really know how to show us that he loved us and admired us for our accomplishments; it was something he kept to himself. Despite any deficiencies in displaying his affection by telling me he loved me or by hugging me or whatever other means of displaying affection you can think of, my Dad has always been there for me when it really counted and his actions stand as the evidence that he does and always has loved me even if he didn't like or understand the things I have done in my life. I spent a big portion of my life chasing after his love and trying to prove myself to him and letting go of this drive was the most difficult thing I ever had to do for myself when I figured out I needed to let go of that and please myself.

CREATIONS OF SOCIETY

In sociology there is much to be said for how the social environment for which a person is disposed shapes their character and so they say that society makes people what they are but what needs to be realized is that society is made up of individuals and so it becomes a which came first the chicken or the egg scenario. The individual is shaped in the social sense by society for the most part but the self-actualizing person has come to the realization that they as a single entity have the power to decide who or what they are to be and so the constraints of society fall away and they are free to design themselves. Becoming educated of this fact is the first step to removing yourself from the chains of enculturation. Since society is made up of single beings it is certainly logical to say that every idea of society and culture had to begin with one person and then grow from them to others before it became something of society and culture. I'm reminded of "The Lottery" by Shirley Jackson. In the story the people of the town gather together every year for a ritual where one person is selected to be stoned to death, yet nobody knows why anymore. It is supposed that the ritual sacrifice was born out of some antiquated religious idea that sacrifice to a god will bring a bountiful crop or good fortune to the town and without the sacrifice bad things will happen, but in the story the people of the town just blindly go along with the ritual without any real reason or understanding of why it is done anymore. This is the way most average people live their lives. They blindly follow along with the rules and conventions of the society and culture they associate with usually from birth and never think to ask why. They never step outside of their life and ask themselves who or what they are as an individual. They are consumed with conforming to the rules and standards that society has placed upon them. They go to church and school and take in what is given to them and spit it out to someone else and pass it along without really tearing it apart and weighing it for themselves. It is the self-actualizing person who has the question awakened within them and desires to know and understand what they are and what they can be and bridge the gap between what they are and what they wish to become. You have the power to overcome the circumstances of your life!

Self-actualizing people have a capacity to appreciate the basic beauty in life that most of us take for granted. Any sunset may be as beautiful as the first one, a single flower may be breath-taking even after seeing a million and a husband can be as enthralled by the beauty of his wife even at sixty years of age just as he was the day he married her. These people find inspiration from the basic experiences in life like children with a fresh set of eyes and none of them will get this same sort of high from parties, money or drugs; it is a natural personal high which has been described by William James as the Mystic Experience. In my explanation it is a feeling of flying like I am not bound to this body or to the world. It is as if I am my soul souring high above the world feeling limitless and powerful; like a god, I dare say. It isn't something I get through church or any other external source of satisfaction; it is something I find within myself as I simply let go of the ties that hold me to the world so to speak; I let go of self. It is transcendence. I cannot seem to find the words for it. It is like death. The dead cannot explain what being dead is like because it is just something which cannot be explained it must be experienced.

Self-actualizing people though they do tend to be detached from society as a whole they do tend to have a profound compassion for all people in general and though their interpersonal relationships are few these few relationships tend to be more profound than average friendships. I thought it was interesting recently while watching a documentary hosted by Alan Alda in his search for the Human

Spark; the thing which makes us different from other animals and makes us uniquely human, when an anthropologist explained to him that apes can mentally manage relationships to about fifty individuals and humans could manage about one-hundred-fifty and the point was that it is because the brain of the human is three times the size of the ape's brain. This point got me to thinking about how if my brain can manage shallow relationships with about one-hundred-fifty people then what would it be like if I had a lot fewer friends to focus all that brain power on. If I only have fifteen friends then it seems logical that I could afford to know them all ten times better than I could know one-hundred-fifty. How much deeper and more meaningful would those relationships be?

Self-actualizing people can be friendly with anyone of suitable character regardless of class, education, age, politics, race, color or religion and seemingly do so without even being aware of these differences that most average people use to profile others and judge the value of possible interaction. They are honestly respectful and humble to anyone who shows the character or talent to teach them something. It is to say they don't judge the value of interaction upon what someone looks like, what they are wearing or how old they are but rather the content of their character as Dr. King suggested we do. They don't get off on putting others down or acting superior or trying to hurt others to get a laugh. That's not to say they can't or won't act hostile towards another, in fact the self-actualizing person will speak harshly of and to those who act hypocritical, pretentious or pompous. The self-actualizing person won't sit idly by and allow one person to attack another person who doesn't have it coming.

Self-actualizing people are driven to creativity. They lack the boundaries of enculturation and tend to express themselves more freely and naturally in every way one can express themselves. Their ability to see a problem or idea objectively without the rules and limitations of culture or ego allow them to focus on not only the good of the ends but on the means as well. They rather see the means as ends and so they derive pleasure not only from the solution/product but also from the doing or the work in solving a problem or creating something. Their creativeness could be compared to the creativeness of a child which hasn't been spoiled by culture or dogma. It is a natural state which we find in us as children but is suppressed through our disposition to culture and educated out of us. When was the last time you looked upon a cloud and said it looks like something other than a cloud? This resistance to enculturation makes one seem as though they are not well adjusted. The self-actualizing person may get along with the culture yet they remain detached from it internally. They are autonomous beings ruled by the laws of their own character wearing a cloak of outer acceptance which seems to be a contrast to the true nature of the self-actualized person. It is as if they are forced by the rule of society to restrain who they truly are for the sake of society. They must lessen their spontaneity to an extent that some of their potentials are not actualized; it seems to be a type of self-contradiction and it probably is. Like I said the self-actualizing person isn't perfect. This is the disorder of my condition and this book is to me a part of the solution. It is my quest for people like me with whom I may associate to relieve me of this burden.

For the average person the world is a dangerous place and is defined by two types of people those he can dominate and those who can dominate him, but the satisfied person can take his needs for granted and devote himself to a higher ideal and greater good. Dichotomies are destroyed when what seems to be contrast is no longer so. When my will and God's will are the same then I can trust my impulses to do good and right. It is no longer thoughtful or arduous, but natural and pleasing to me. I am unselfish out of selfishness and my duty/work is my pleasure and brings me great joy; I will love God and do as I will.

BEING AN INDIVIDUAL

I would like to try to define individuality through an understanding of the definition of the words which make up the word individuality. It is an interesting way to look at things sometimes and I can always find a meaning which I tend to think is the original purpose of a word but is simply forgotten over time and the true meaning is lost to what society or culture tends to think of a word without really examining it.

For example the meaning of hypothesis; hypo means weak or lacking strength or validity and thesis means an argument or idea, so hypothesis is a weak argument which is a fitting definition for what hypothesis really is which most people's idea of what hypothesis means is kind of uncertain and seems more complicated than it needs to be.

Individuality is a great word and I can find some interesting definitions to its pieces which make perfect sense for what I am trying to convey in this book. Think of indivisible which means that something which is undivided and cannot be divided because of its strength and duality reminds me of the duality of man from Jungian perspective of psychology. Duality of man is the concept of the good and evil of what man is in that we can create and destroy in equal measure and seemingly through our actions as a species we tend to do both. We destroy ourselves through war for the purpose of creating peace which seems to be a contradiction. I will stick with the idea that duality is simply the good and evil of a person and that when the good and evil are understood by the person and they are fully understanding of the good and evil within themselves and bring the duality together they become undivided. So it is to say that the duality of a person becomes undivided. This is a person who is honest and fully aware of all the good and evil they possess; all the potential of what they can be, and are unafraid of what they are. Most average people don't achieve this because we are taught to ignore, suppress and be afraid of anything of us which may be evil.

THE WILL TO KILL

A conscientious objector is someone who claims that they are unable to provide service to the military because they believe they cannot under any circumstances take the life of another human being. I gave a lot of thought to this idea when I was younger and questioned whether or not I could take another life and thought very long and hard even to the point of imagining the act itself so vividly as to try to understand how I would feel after I had killed someone. I even imagined not as a circumstance of self-defense or self-preservation but simply as the murder of someone. I found myself going through a sort of pacifistic phase in my early twenties which I grew out of pretty quickly after getting my head knocked around a bit at a couple of parties I attended. I remember from Orson Scott Card's *Ender's Game* when the main character comes to the conclusion that "the only power that really matters in life is the power to kill and those without that power or ability will always be subject to those who have that power or ability. Those who cannot kill are subject to those who can.". The point is the will to determine your rights and power to enforce them define the limits of your rights.

I have contemplated the animal drives; instincts within every animal in the world and come to the conclusion that the ultimate drives were rather simple. Survival of the individual and survival of the species; survival of the species is related to our natural animal drives to procreate, to spread our seed and this cannot happen without the survival of the individual. So I came up with the idea that if one were to sacrifice their own survival for the survival of another, this would be the ultimate act of being more than an animal. It is as the bible says no greater love than the one who lays down his life for another. So is anyone truly a conscientious objector? I think it is possible but it is something so rare that it hardly deserves much discussion, because the will to sacrifice your life for someone else doesn't necessarily mean you would just let someone else kill you when you have the means to defend yourself and I think no matter who you are or how deeply you believe you couldn't kill someone if you're pushed hard enough and if the threat is great enough your instincts will take over and you will do what you must; it is only natural.

Taking another life is a horrible thing of course but if we are to condemn the act as the ultimate form of evil and condition people to believe that there is no circumstance of which killing is to be accepted or understood then we condemn ourselves and especially the people we charge with defending our country to misery and insanity. Again it is a conditioning/enculturation of our minds to the norms/values of society to a point where the individual is no more. If you think the actions of our government are out of your hands and you wish to think yourself quite unaccountable for what is done by it then you are a fool. The blood is on your hands just as much as anyone else's.

LOVE IN SELF-ACTUALIZING PEOPLE

We must understand love; we must be able to teach it, to create it, to predict it, or else the world is lost to hostility and suspicion.

—Abraham Maslow

As I have stated earlier every relationship is made of three basic interaction characteristics; honesty, trust and communication. With these characteristics being the foundation for the relationship over time if these characteristics are strong then love and commitment to the relationship will develop quite naturally. In our just add water, high speed world it seems as though love has become something of an overnight quick fix for the average normal person. Most average relationships are based upon the fulfillment of a deficiency from one person to another. It is a needing of another person to provide personal social stimulus which cannot be fulfilled otherwise and one cannot get along without. We here all the time about how the divorce rate is getting higher and higher all the time. Couples are on television talking to Dr. Phil about the deficiencies of their relationships and how to fix things. They don't communicate enough or are not being honest with their partner or don't trust their partner. This has become the norm of our society. Marriage and love have become something of a quick fix instant coffee mix and if it starts to go sour you just get a divorce and move on to the next unfulfilling marriage or relationship.

Everybody wants to go a hundred miles an hour with their hair on fire in their relationship and swear to themselves and to this other person that we are meant to be and destined to be as if it was planned by God so ultimately we can make the excuse that if it didn't work it wasn't meant to be and it is no fault of our own. It was all part of God's plan to put us through an emotional wringer to teach us some sort of lesson we couldn't figure out for ourselves otherwise only to turn around and do it all over again with the next person. We want to believe that God has made some particular person with whom we are destined to be with in his perfect plan for our lives because we want to think it is a beautiful thing that God loves us so much he would create someone to be our very own love.

Let's think about that for a minute. God created someone to be your property? Is that what you're trying to say? I don't buy it! The truth and beauty of it; love is a choice not a feeling. Life isn't planned for you. You are a being of free will and responsible for all your mistakes and triumphs of your own. The beauty of it is that if someone chooses to be with you they are giving you something of themselves. It's not some fairy tale life we live in. The actions you take have consequences both good and bad. It's just like the money in your pocket; you can't spend that dollar on one thing if you first spend it on another; you give up one thing in order to attain something else. That feeling you have inside for someone you think is love is really attachment or desire for attachment or worse, desire for control which in and of itself is fear. Most people jump the gun and want to be in a hurry to feel secure in their relationship and have that desire for attachment fulfilled so they do the one thing they can do to try to resolve it; they say "I love you". It's not really a statement it's a question most of the time even with the normal healthy minded person. When it comes to love relationships I think is a rare condition to be of a healthy mind. When it comes to love I am fairly convinced we are infected as a society to be rather confused and disoriented. We don't as a society understand what it really is or how to create it. The word love for its true intent and purpose has lost its meaning as a word anymore. It's just a word which sounds nice and is used to manipulate others.

It is an interesting note of difference between the average person and the self-actualizing person as found by Maslow in his studies of love that the self-actualizing person doesn't say it much at all and only to or about a rare few people in their life. In love relationships between self-actualizing people there are some unique findings in Maslow's studies. They don't tend to feel anxiety about being separated from their loved one, they don't feel jealous or suspicious of their partner's time apart or other relationships with friends, they don't worry about their partner's faults or weaknesses, they don't get bored with each other and the sex just seems to get better all the time. These relationships are rich in spontaneity and honesty in that these people don't feel they need to front or hide who they truly are. They are for all intents and purposes free and natural with one another.

According to Maslow when a person is satisfied in their physiological and safety needs they will find a new center of their universe. They will feel the absence of friends or a partner and children to share their good fortune. We are not talking about sex. Sex is a purely physiological drive. We are talking about love. Love is about giving and taking. One must have the power to love and the capacity to be loved as it is giving and receiving. You can love someone all you want; it doesn't make them love you back. Many relationships in this day seem to fall short here. There is great confusion in this area of social needs. Many people get love confused with belongingness or acceptance. They cling to someone out of fear instead of love.

Fear of being alone and of instability especially concerning the condition of single parenthood is a bad reason for seeking companionship. As important or advantageous as it may be to have a normal two parent home and two incomes to the household and more hands to get the laundry done, it doesn't do anything positive if you're spending time wooing a partner when your kids need you. If you can manage it responsibly that is great and I wish you the best just be careful about your motives because it's easy to get mixed up.

Know your motivations. Know yourself. I am a single parent myself and I have been down that road. My opinion is that my child is my number one priority in my life and I place myself second to him. It is unfair and unrealistic for me to expect a potential partner to fill any role regarding my son or to fill a role for me without consideration of him as well. I have been involved with women who adored him and liked me ok; it doesn't work. I have been involved with women who placed these expectations on themselves; it doesn't work. I have been involved with women who adored me and were competitive with my son for my time and attention; that won't work. Worst of all is my fault in the matter because I have tried to fulfill a desire for something in my life with something that doesn't work. The little wisdom I have salvaged from this is the opinion that until my son is old enough that he doesn't need me so much I really don't need to be trying to get too serious with anybody. This is a fine notion because it works for me and allows me the opportunity to be patient. I do go on dates occasionally but I prefer to call them informal meetings as a reminder to me and to my date to just relax and be natural. No pressure. No expectations. Take your time.

Love isn't some mysterious cloud that falls from the sky. There is no one particular person with whom you are destined or planned to connect to; your life isn't planned out by God as this idea is contrary to free will. Love is a choice to harness an individual internal force and manifest it into action. If you tell someone you love them and expect them to return the favor then you weren't truly expressing love at all. If you do something for someone and expect something in return your action wasn't motivated by love. Love has nothing to do with your status in life, how you look, the car you drive, the job you hold, wealth or lack of it; these factors are in no way a good measure of someone's potential as a partner. You have to be ever vigilant and objective of yourself when dealing with love. Love should come naturally in time from an ever increasing quantity of honesty, trust and communication between two people. Two people who truly love one another would be well aware of each other's faults and shortcomings and still be in love.

If you find yourself hiding something about yourself or evoking a persona that isn't naturally who you are then you need to spend some time working on you and coming to terms of self-acceptance because you cannot truly accept someone else's faults if you can't accept yours. If you feel that your potential partner is being fake with you, just give it time. One can only keep up their stage character for so long. Eventually when push comes to shove the real person they are will rear their ugly head. I'm not saying it is grounds for a split but this person obviously needs to deal with their own inner demons and again accept themselves before they can be truly honest with you and if you can't deal with their faults then maybe you need to look at yourself as well.

I'm reminded of my Aunt Mary and Uncle Larry. They have been together since they were kids and they are now into their sixties. I have spent enough time with them over the years to see they fit together quite well as I hesitate to use the word perfect, but they are as close to it as I think you can get. I have seen either one of them irritated with something the other does so neither one of them is blind to the faults of the other, but it is at these times I see them instead of fussing about it simply smile and shrug it off and it is gone like magic as if it never mattered. It is at these times I see them instead being constructively supportive of one another to gently guide the other in another direction so to speak. I have also seen that spark in each of them that tells you they are still very much in love with one another. It is a rare and wonderful thing and I have always admired them for their relationship with each other and the encouragement they give to others. They are excellent hosts and infectious personalities; I wish I could visit them more often. They are the best example I know of what a marriage can and should be. They haven't had it easy either. Larry's job kept him away from home for long hours and they've had all the ups and downs that come with managing a home and a family that anyone has. They made their marriage what it is by the strength of their backs and the sweat of their brows.

A friend once told me that a successful marriage is simply a matter of finding someone you can live with who will put up with your shit. Sounds fairly simple and easy and maybe to some it reeks of settling, but I don't think so. I think it is the same to say each person must be comfortable with who they are and accepting of themselves. If you are accepting of yourself and your faults it is much easier to accept others for their imperfections. If you are aware of your own faults then it is easier to appreciate the fact that your partner is willing to put up with you; this should be quite satisfying. When you know who someone is and can trust them to be who they are because they come to you as naturally as they can be and if you can do the same then it is easy to build a relationship. If you can trust someone to not judge you then it is easy to communicate and be honest and through honest communication you build more trust so it is a self-building cycle. The opposite is true if these relationship characteristics is flawed, so if you or your partner are lacking then the relationship isn't true and will fall apart in due time or it will come to a head as my Dad would say.

If someone loves you or if you love someone, of course it is nice to hear it but to speak it shouldn't be necessary. You should treat the object of your affection in such a manner that they need never hear you say it. You should know whether or not someone loves you by the way they treat you. To truly love someone requires you to know the worst thing about them there is to know and still you love them without pause. I'm not saying to refrain from uttering those three little words; it is nice to hear it, just don't use it as a substitute for action. You can't judge someone's care for you based upon what they say they feel. If what they say they feel doesn't compel them to action then it is just bullshit; no other word better describes it.

People use the word love as a tool of manipulation; as a means to control someone else. Be wary of people who say it allot, it's a good indicator of their own insecurities. If you are mindful of the circumstances of your surroundings you can often figure out their true motivation for saying at that particular moment and it usually has more to do with control and territorialism than love. I see it all the time. A couple is in a social setting such as a bar or a park and because of their insecurities regarding the strength of their relationship in the face of say a potential rival; in the animal sense;

a man or woman will embrace their partner and display affection not for the sake of affection but as a message to others and for the security of reciprocation. This is not the nature of true love.

True love is to love without reservation or fear. As Jesus was denied by Peter, who will you deny when faced with the option to die if you don't deny? Peter's fault was his lack of understanding what true love is, but I'm fairly certain or at least I hope that he came to better understanding of it through this experience. Was it wrong for Peter to deny his friend? In the scope of the big picture; not really because nothing of importance was to be gained at that moment for Peter or for anyone else and much was at risk if he didn't do so; Jesus' prediction of Peter's denial wasn't because Peter wasn't able to control himself or his life but because it was only the natural thing to do in the circumstance.

INDIVIDUAL RIGHTS AND CRIMINALITY

The English common people established their rights through The English Bill of Rights of 1689; nearly one-hundred years prior to our Declaration of Independence. The English Bill of Rights wasn't passed through a peaceful process either but at the threat of revolt. The Englishmen stood ready, sword in hand to take what he believed to be his by divine proclamation. Only thoses who are willing to take action to attain what they believe they deserve truly deserve a thing. Only those who are willing to do whatever is necessary to attain and defend a thing deserve the thing. The Bill of Rights of the Constitution of the United States is only a piece of paper with some words on it. It is not required to define what our rights should be and certainly doesn't cover all the rights one should enjoy. No piece of paper or signature is necessary to the protection of our rights; only the willful exercise of those rights is necessary to establish them. We have adopted a false doctrine in this country of the belief that what is written is the law and defines what is right.

It is a strange practice I think; the taking away of the right to vote from any person who commits a felony. What is the commission of crime if not an argument with the law and a vote against such law? We have become an unforgiving nation. If one makes a mistake even as a young immature person such a mistake, thanks to technology, will follow them and stifle their liberties and opportunities for the rest of their lives. For the purposes of this conversation let's leave the most grotesque criminal acts out of this equation for a moment and think of non-violent crimes. Laws are enacted as a means to eliminate some sort of ill we believe to be plaguing society. Usually these means are a matter of relinquishment of personal liberties because we find a condition that the average individual isn't to be trusted to manage their own liberty so we leave it to society (governance) to manage it for us through some type of prohibition. We create laws to inhibit a one's ability to attain or utilize a resource and make criminals of them when they violate these prohibitions. If one is incapable of managing their liberties due to their own ignorance, the solution shouldn't be to take away the liberty it should be to educate them so that they may more readily and competently manage their own liberty. By taking the action to limit the liberties of all because the majority is found to be incompetent we condemn those who are of sound mind and judgment to a life less lived and condemn the majority to ignorance. My desire is that every human person should enjoy a life rich in liberty to fully realize their own potential to become what they are. On the other hand someone is isn't ignorant of the good judgment necessary to manage their liberties and chooses to neglect their responsibility and it causes suffering to others should have those liberties restrained and the offender should be applied to a process of restoring themselves to society. Our criminal justice system as it is has nothing to do with justice and does nothing to restore the victim or the offender to society. There is no true system of reform within our criminal justice system and the notion of paying a debt to society through serving time in prison is absurd. The debt which needs to be paid should be to the victim and the offender needs to be put to a process which eventually restores their life to the liberties of citizenship.

Someone who is convicted of a felony crime related to drug possession not only loses their right to vote but is also denied financial assistance opportunities for higher education. This is an absurd policy and needs to be addressed! What hope do these people have of changing their stars without a chance to get an education? Most of these people are from lower income and lesser educated areas. So what else is left for them to do but continue to be criminals? Not only have we taken away their right to vote against or protest the laws which have oppressed them, but we strip away their hopes of ever attaining a better life through any means. We have condemned them to a hell we have designed for them in the first place. As if their lives weren't to be difficult enough for the fact they must carry with them a criminal record which condemns them as a person who can never be trusted, but we destroy the chance for them to restore themselves to society at all. In my studies as well as the studies of others concerning crime rates within the United States the key correlating factor is referred to as social economic status. It is a combination of variables concerning economics and education of a given population area. Crime rates within areas of a lower factor social economic status tend to be higher. It is no wonder that crime rates would be higher in areas which lack economic and education opportunities. It could easily be concluded that access to education is the primary variable because the economic picture of an area can likely be changed if people are educated to be able to create opportunities to improve economic conditions through the creation of private sector jobs by starting businesses. A person who is convicted of dealing marijuana doesn't need to go to prison; they need to get a business degree.

Since most of you will refer to the constitution for the determination of your rights, we should have a look at some of them. Only the first, second and ninth actually protect individual rights by making allowances to the people and the rest work by providing prohibitions against the government. I have great issue with the government restrictions upon the first and second amendments for this very reason. Whether you realize it or not we have found ourselves in a time when these rights no longer mean anything. The Patriot Act is the most recent legislation which has dissolved the rights promised by the constitution and more legislation is on the way which is being written again in the name of protecting us from an enemy who hasn't even targeted us as an enemy yet. This new legislation will open up the books of corporations to law enforcement for the purposes of finding any monetary ties to terrorist organizations which seems like a good idea even though it will violate the privacy of every other individual who may be invested in those companies. I'm sure we will be hearing more about the dirty dealings of our own politicians and campaign finance fraud as a result of this new law if it is enacted; quite a damaging blow by the democratic party to the republicans I'm sure. Hit them where it hurts; in the wallet.

The first amendment is the promise of the right to speak out, to petition, to argue with anything we see as wrong. The right to vote is the mark of this right and the proof of citizenship. If one isn't a citizen then he must be either a sovereign or a slave. So by stripping away one's right to vote we make slaves of them. Who shall we take this right from next? It is dangerous ground for any reason to attempt to limit free speech. The old saying, "give them an inch and they'll take a mile" is precisely what we risk to happen if we draw any limitations on any right. I work in a restaurant and the wait staff is required to wear black shoes. These shoes are not to have any other color patterns on them at all. Someone shows up one day with a pair of shoes which have a thin white stripe about a quarter inch wide and if the manager allows this the next thing you know someone shows up with a half inch stripe then an inch. Next thing you know everyone is wearing shoes with varying width white stripes on them. It is the same thing with our other rights. If we place any kind of limit no matter how small on a right we open the door for more and more limits until we have no right at all. Because of the information age and the 24-7 news machine insignificant people and groups of people with the worst ideas are getting massive amounts of attention. Because of the audacity of these ideas and the potential hazard it may pose in eliciting a violent response from certain groups of people who may take offense we are tempted to try to draw some kind of limit to free speech. The fact is however that anyone who would take violent action over some idea posed by a radical are no less radical than those who offended them.

GUN CONTROL AND INDIVIDUAL RIGHTS

The second amendment is the promise of the possession of arms for one to defend themselves, their family and neighbors from any entity which make seek to violate their rights. Through the course of my investigation of the subject of gun control and its' effect on crime I developed an added perspective to include not only its' impact upon crime but also its' impact upon individual rights. After noting the fallout of gun control in England as stated by Joyce Malcolm in her article *Gun Control's Twisted Outcome* and her *Lessons of History: Firearms Regulations and the Reduction of Crime* I have decided to take a deeper look into the gun debate in the U.S. and have found the same lack of logic that shaped public policy in England to be shaping policy here. I find it disturbing to say the least that legislators will act without hesitation to baseless ideas while completely ignoring factual information. This lack of logic in our governance has led to many problems we are now facing and seem destined to face in the future. My original intent was to discover on my own through my own search for truth to determine where I stand on this issue. I have come to the conclusion that I believe myself to be in agreement with the founding fathers and the philosophers who have shaped their beliefs. I cannot, no matter what any law says relinquish myself of the natural responsibility to defend myself, my home and my neighbors from harm. I couldn't in good conscience walk down the street and ignore someone being attacked and leave it to someone else to act simply because I don't have a badge. So I cannot sit idly by and allow the liberties I hold dear to be threatened by false doctrine. For all their good intentions the anti-gun lobby has a misled agenda. We can all agree to do everything possible to take guns away from criminality, but to take them away from law abiding citizens is to leave the weak at the mercy of the strong. Criminals do prefer unarmed victims and those in power prefer unarmed subjects. Based upon the sources I have found in my search for an answer to the gun debate, I would have to side with favoring less gun control as a means to lower crime rates and I fear political action and legislation of more stringent gun laws which infringe upon citizens' rights to self-protection against criminals and the government as the apparent result is a road to fewer and fewer liberties. My personal opinion of the matter would be to require every citizen to be required to complete firearms training certification and leave it alone after that. Law abiding citizens should need no restrictions upon the type of arms they may own or carry with them. Those who claim that reason must be applied to limits forget that reason is a matter for the individual as a part of society and is determined by individuals as a part of society. No law should then be needed to dictate to anyone what is reasonable. Law abiding citizens should be trusted to determine on their own what is reasonable; this is the point of view from which our constitution was founded. Denying the liberties protected by the Bill of Rights finds no solution to the problems of crime and violence. In fact it is found that societies which fail to respect these Natural Rights John Locke refers to suffer from not only higher crime rates but also higher incidence of degradative ills and eventual political and social breakdown and upheaval. The reason for this is it is impossible to keep weapons out of the hands of those who choose to disregard the law. Locked doors only keep honest people honest and laws only keep law-abiding citizens from doing a thing which the law prohibits. So the law therefore only serves to limit the potential of those who choose to live a life of responsibility to society as we take weapons out of the hands of those who should have them as a flawed means of trying to remove them from criminals and those who would commit evil acts with them.

Without question, our founders were well aware of these dangers and were clear in their intent to protect these liberties.

The National Rifle Association-Institute for Legislative Action (NRA-ILA) suggests, according to their website, crime rates for any given state are reduced significantly in states allowing citizens to carry concealed firearms on their person for the purposes of personal defense. The Violence Policy Center (VPC) claims, a higher gun ownership rate determines the rates of violent crime.

Uniform Crime Reports (UCR) data which is collected by the FBI annually, shows a significant reduction in crime overall in the U.S. during the last 20 years, but the reasons for it are not significantly clear to me having already compared data concerning Law Enforcement Employment Rates to Population changes and economic indicators such as Gross Domestic Product, Unemployment and Population Growth Rates. Other potential variables I have yet to examine are Sociological Theories concerning Racial and Ethnic Relations, Religious Ideology in Social Bonding, Public Attitudes towards Law Enforcement, Quality of Law Enforcement, Administrative Policies in Law Enforcement, Social Justice Programs and Technological Advancements. Any or all of these factors as well as others may have attributed to the decline in crime in the U.S., it is difficult to determine which factors have had the greatest or most efficient impact and I think it may be speculative at best for one to say a single factor was the key. Ultimately my research purpose would be to attempt to quantify the direct impact of changes in Gun Control on Crime Rates. Focusing on one state will help to minimize the differences in social factors effect on data comparison.

According to the NRA-ILA website, the State of Missouri passed its CCW Right to Carry (RTC) in September of 2003 by override of Governor Bob Holden's veto of HB 349, making Missouri the 36th state to pass a RTC law. In more recent developments the Missouri House passed an amendment allowing concealed weapons on college campuses; the bill has been sitting on Governor Jay Nixon's desk for consideration since May 25th.

According to Professor John Lott's research into the subject of Gun Control in the U.S. in his report *When Gun Control Costs Lives*, no statistical data can be found to support the notion of fewer guns means less crime; his studies show quite the opposite. His research shows, taking guns away from law abiding citizens puts them at risk to be victims to crime that otherwise could have been neutralized. In his research Lott also finds that every other aspect noted by gun control advocates such as suicide, family crimes and accidental shootings are relatively low and unaffected by gun regulations. Most importantly no gun laws no matter how stringent have any effect on stopping criminals from attaining and using guns in crimes; they are criminals and criminals don't abide the law. According to Lott no action such as firearm registration, gun lock and storage laws, gun show laws or waiting periods show any benefit while in contrast laws which enforce the individual right to self-protection through Right-to Carry laws show impacts which are all too often ignored by the public media.

It is difficult to see the distinction in the current state of gun control affairs in the U.S. Joyce Malcolm shows in her research reports *Gun Control's Twisted Outcome* and *History: Firearms Regulations and the Reduction of Crime* the impact on crime and rights of citizens of ever tightening gun control laws in Great Britain. She shows us through the history of England's gun control up to present day how crime rates have risen to the highest levels not only experienced by the English but comparatively the highest crime rates of the industrialized world. She points out that the English citizen has no rights at all to self-protection from criminals and criminals not only enjoy free reign to terrorize the public, they can actually file suit against a victim if they are injured if a victim attempts to defend themselves and the government will pay for the legal fees to file the suit. Malcolm explains that American common law and rights concerning self-protection and helping your neighbor are concepts inherited from England. She goes on to point out that when comparing data between the U.S. and Britain it is significant to note UCR statistics for murder include cases of justifiable homicide and self-defense while English stats are calculated based upon the clear outcome of non-justifiable homicide so that the murder rate appears to be lower in Britain, but the reality is quite converse. She also shows

73

us the criminal mentality in the data comparison; 53% of burglaries in Britain occur whilst the home is occupied to 13% in the U.S. where burglars fear armed homeowners. Malcolm points out that legislative action to abolish gun ownership rights in Britain were reactive to specific incidents of gun violence and public outrage as a means to appear to be doing something about the problem instead of being based upon any substantial evidence to support the idea that such action would reduce crime. Malcolm points out England didn't even have a professional police force until the 1830s and up until then relied upon citizens to police themselves as the principles of common law expected people to protect themselves and their neighbors. She also notes the passage of the *Firearms Control Act of 1920* was passed for fear of revolution in the wake of World War I not crime at all.

In their research report, *Does Gun Control Reduce Crime or Does Crime Increase Gun Control,* John Moorhouse and Brent Wanner find, through comprehensive analysis of multi-variable regressive study of crime rates, no evidence at all that restrictive gun laws reduce crime, but find that crime induces legislative response in the form of gun control. Their data shows that the most likely areas to react with the passage of gun restrictions as a notion to reduce crime are those with people of better education levels, higher per capita income and higher percentage of democrats in state legislature. So basically, the very people who should be and claim to be looking at the issue from a purely academic point of view are taking action based on a false pretense. This is in my opinion a warning sign of things to come when it is related to Malcolm's research. What other rights are we willing to give up in the name of crime control only to find ourselves defenseless against not only criminals but politicians and governance that acts in ignorance and falsely promises to protect us while not allowing us to protect ourselves?

In his *Newsweek* article *The Changing Gun Debate*, New York Mayor Michael Bloomberg suggests a pragmatic approach to the issue. He notes the question shouldn't be about law abiding citizen rights to gun ownership and rights to defend ones' self, it should simply be a point we can all agree upon; getting guns out of the hands of criminals. Bloomberg says the congress of the U.S. has made it impossible for local law enforcement to track down the sources of illegal weapons by keeping necessary information out of the hands of law enforcement. He calls for national action to a national problem. While I agree with Bloomberg's approach and notion to keep guns away from criminals, I believe national policy on the matter to be unnecessary. The federal government is sloppy and inefficient in its handling of a multitude of other matters and I don't believe we are in need of more blanket laws as what works in one state may not be effective in another. Bloomberg notes sting operations which have caught gun dealers violating the law. This is something local law enforcement can do on its own without requiring congress to create another commission or administration to waste tax payers law enforcement dollars on; we don't need more administrators in offices wasting tax dollars on feel good programs, we need more cops on the street.

A recent Supreme Court Decision in the case of *McDonald v. Chicago* made it clear that the second amendment applies to states. The Violence Policy Center Legislative Director Kristen Rand claims that people will die because of this decision. She and her organization claim that gun ownership is a deadly proposition. She claims that the family gun is to blame for murder-suicides, family violence, and mass shootings. Lott points out that the data collected for the Violence Policy Center only counted deaths that occurred in homes that owned firearms and made no note of the fact that the deaths were caused not by the family firearm but by the firearms the invader brought. Don Kates and Gary Mauser in their study *Would Banning Firearms Reduce Murder and Suicide* show a large comparative study of nations worldwide the correlation between murder and suicide to more guns doesn't exist. They go on to point out that people kill themselves for reasons they deem sufficient and in the absence of firearms they kill themselves in some other way. In *Second Thoughts About Gun Control*, James Wright, a former gun control advocate, says research doesn't show that strict gun controls can curb illegal gun use and in the case of a ban, black market supplies would still be available. He goes on to note that arguments for stricter gun control fail every empirical test and none of the laws enacted significantly reduced the rate of criminal violence. In the NRA-ILA *Right to Carry 2010* the right to self-defense has been recognized for centuries. The U.S Supreme Court in *U.S. v Cruikshank* (1876) recognized that, "The right to arms is an individual right and that it is not a right granted by the constitution and isn't in any manner dependent upon the constitution for its existence.". The idea that citizens should leave their safety to the police has been struck down by the courts as well in *Warren v. District of Columbia* (1981), the D.C. court of appeals ruled, "police personnel and the government employing them aren't liable to victims of criminal acts for failure to provide adequate police protection; the government and its agents are under no general duty to provide public services, such as police protection, to any particular citizen.". Anti-gun researcher David McDowell's study *Easing Concealed Firearms Laws: Effects on Homicide in Three States* claimed that gun homicide rates increased in Miami, Jacksonville and Tampa after Florida's 1987 RTC law, but he used data from the early 1970s to calculate data for Jacksonville and Tampa when homicide rates were lower than in 1993 and used 1983 data for Miami in his comparison again when rates were lower. None of McDowell's homicides was committed by a RTC permit holder. The truth of the data from UCR is a decline in homicide rates after the RTC law by 10% in Miami, 18% in Jacksonville and 20% in Tampa between 1987 and 1993.

The most recent piece of legislation pertaining to RTC in Missouri is a bill on Governor Jay Nixon's desk waiting to be signed since May 25, 2010. The bill will allow concealed carry permit holding students to carry on college campuses and lowers the permit age requirement to 21. This bill has no doubt stirred the pot for anti-gun folks. MU Chief of Police Jack Watring said at a faculty meeting that he opposed the legislation. He cited his biggest concern would be the tactical problems it would create such as the ability for police to identify a suspect in a situation where many people are carrying weapons. As a former police officer I can offer Chief Watring a piece of advice from my training: Identify yourself before you take action as the law requires you to do. The bad guy will be the one who points his gun at you and the law abiding student will be the one helping to defend himself, his fellow students and you. Many House members said the purpose of this new bill is to provide extra protection in the incident of a shooting like the 2007 Virginia Tech rampage.

We cannot have this debate without including the founding principles of our government. In *Two Treatises of Government* John Locke through philosophical argument attests that power of government regardless of whether it is monarch or representative or any other form is found in the consent of the governed. According to Locke each of us is our own governor and Lord of our own domain and enters into agreement with society for the preservation of our natural rights to life, liberty and property. These natural rights are the foundation of our government and were the primary concern of protection for our founding fathers. It is this same principle of natural rights that has led us to abolish slavery, enact civil rights legislation and leads our ideals as Americans to reach out to others whose rights are threatened in every place of the world. Without these rights we have no commission of authority to argue with the practices of cruel and unusual punishments by stoning to death women in Iran, or the torture of prisoners in China, or the incarceration and punishment of people without fair trial. What will we base our argument on if we give up these rights? If we give up one right, what will we use as our argument for the protection of other rights which are based upon the same principles? If say the right to bear arms which is founded upon the same principle as free speech and liberty then to what principle will we look to for defense of these rights? It is clear that once any one of these rights is stripped away the others will not be far behind. Without the Second Amendment Right we have no defense to our other rights.

UNDERSTANDING 9/11 AND ITS IMPLICATIONS

The Patriot Act was a consequence of the fear response to the terrorist attacks of 9/11. We have sacrificed our liberties for the hope of gaining security. The fact is however that sacrificing liberty is a sacrifice of security. The reasons the terrorists were able to pull off such a magnificent attack was a result of our lack of will to act appropriately. The first failure was the lax and inconsistent screening policies of the aviation industry. Realistically though; what kind of a weapon is a box knife? The second and most important failure was the lack of resolve of the average citizen to take responsibility to act in the defense of themselves and their neighbor. We had been trained to just go along and don't fight back. We expected the government to deal with the situation and protect us from harm. So in the moment of truth when action was necessary we failed to act because it is what we had been conditioned to do. So instead of someone or everyone getting out of their seats and kicking some terrorist ass the people on those planes did what they were expected to do. Let's be realistic about things. If someone threatens me with a box knife, he's getting a beat down. In fact I tell you if someone threatens me with a gun I am confident I can take it away from them and if it is a functioning weapon and is loaded they will probably get shot in the face before I am done removing it from their hands. If someone pulled that crap on a plane now he'd get the stuffing knocked out of him and would be lucky to make it out alive. As tragic as the loss of life and as significant as it was for the level of destruction it entailed; it was a single isolated incident. The kneejerk reaction of the public and politicians to go to war and pass the Patriot Act was hardly appropriate action. We prosecuted two fronts of supposedly the same war against terrorism and surrendered our civil protections against our own government with virtually no deliberation. We bankrupted our country and the return on our investment is no more promising than before we began. We've lost thousands of U.S. service members with nothing to show for it. The whole thing was truly nothing more than a welcome to the world. We helped create this world of hatred and suspicion through our flawed international policies and practices. We just did whatever we wanted however we wanted with no regard for how it was affecting these other people until it came to our doors. It didn't matter as long as Americans were making money on it. It is just the same story as the Columbine High School incident in that those who were affected were introduced to a real phenomenon of life elsewhere we had chosen to ignore. We chose to be naïve and ignore the evil in the world the same way we choose to ignore the evil within ourselves with the false belief that if we ignore it, it will go away. We have made a mess for ourselves and destroyed millions of lives through our self-righteous behavior and solidified the divisions between ourselves and peace. Don't forget that someone somewhere got filthy rich off of all of this.

The end result of our expenditure of blood and treasure is two countries full of people who themselves remain divided over their own religious doctrines, just as they have been for quite a long time, with no discernable positive outcome. It may have been better for everyone involved to have left the whole thing alone because we may have created more problems than we solved. We have spent the majority of the time we have been there trying to determine and exit strategy. Apparently it is easier to get in than to get out. It will be a miracle if these regions don't erupt into civil war the minute we finally get out.

Right now as I am writing this we are posturing with the intent of taking action against Iran for its nuclear weapons programs while at the same time we are laying the foundation for a factory to build parts for nuclear weapons of our own. It is illogical to think that every person in Iran is a terrorist or wishes us harm. These weapons we build if they are used will make no distinction between those who are against us and those who are not. Anyone who is threatened will choose to resist their aggressor. So it is to be expected that the more aggressively we deal with these people the more of them we force to take up actions against us. When will it be enough? If we don't stop this ride and take a look around at where we are and where we seem to be going it is only a matter of time before we drive right off the cliff and into oblivion.

The rights we have surrendered as a result of the passage of the Patriot Act are found in the First, Fourth, Fifth, Sixth and Seventh Amendments. The Fourth Amendment protection from unreasonable search and seizure and the Fifth Amendment protection of property are done away with as federal agents now have the authority to write their own search warrants based upon whatever criteria they deem to search your house for whatever they wish and take whatever they want. The Nazis did this sort of thing. The First Amendment right to free speech is violated as you being the subject of this warrantless search are prohibited from discussing the matter with the press, an attorney or a judge under threat of being convicted to prison for doing so. Trials of matters pertaining to the property seized may be held in secret courts without juries to hear them and you very well might be held without notification of what you are being charged with if you are being charged with anything at all; these actions are violations of the Sixth and Seventh Amendments. Adding all of this together with the fact the Second Amendment has already been limited in that you are restricted to owning only certain types of arms and we can easily make the case that we have no rights in this country any more. We have subjected ourselves to a machine of our own device. This story is for another day. The point is we have become what we are as a society because we have neglected to take responsibility our own lives and thoughts which drive us. Instead of doing what is necessary for ourselves as individuals we have become complacent to allow society and pills to do our thinking for us. We are a nation of dependents.

I deeply appreciate the hard work, effort and intent of those who have served in our military forces because I know why they do it. However I don't see that the actions they have been directed to execute to have provided any more security to our nation in any sense. I have been told they are fighting for my freedom, but I don't need anyone to do that for me. I will fight for my own freedom if I find it being threatened. If I am not willing to defend my rights as a human being by exercising those rights then I deserve no rights. If people want to go around knocking off dictators and regimes and rebuilding countries then they should construct their own private military company and spend their own money to do it. We need to stop interfering in the affairs of other nations. The interests we have served haven't had anything to do with the security of the rights of the individual American. It has been a service to international business interests; the rich exploiting the poor and middle class, and they have used our need for safety as the point to motivate us to action. The truth is there is nothing we can do to stop radicals from taking opportunities to attack us; we can only try to minimize the opportunities. Anyone who trades liberty for security doesn't deserve either because if we sacrifice our liberty then there is no point of security. What are we securing if we fail to secure our liberties? You can't say we are fighting for liberty if our fight requires us to relinquish liberty because in this case we have already lost the fight. If our means to fight injustice are unjust then we haven't secured justice at all.

CONSERVITIVE, LIBERAL OR SOMETHING DIFFERENT

In our 24-7 world of news and information a lot is made for arguments from conservative and liberal viewpoints on life and politics. Not much is said for the view of the average citizen and not many choices are offered on ballots of a different view. Former President Clinton operated on a different philosophy of politics which found him at odds with not only his opposition in the Republican Party but also with his own; Democratic Party. Most people fail to see the relevance of this school of thought from which he led or clearly understand what his motivations were. It is an understanding that we need an effective, accountable and cost efficient government to manage things which can only be managed by government which serves to empower the people and the private sector to prosper by their own hands. It is a progressive approach based upon the understanding of the changing dynamics of the world. Because of the realization of the information age, which is a natural evolution of the world and human kind, now more than ever before in history individuals have the means to realize their potential to speak and share their thoughts, opinions, creativity and character; their voice, with the world. Those who think their vote doesn't matter simply haven't taken the opportunity to tap into this potential. The power of the individual voice is potentially greater than any ballot box they may stand in front of. That is to say that your vote isn't the only tool you have at your disposal to speak your mind. This is the power of the technology we hold in our hands every day now. Seventeen years ago when Clinton took office not many people had mobile phones and there were only a handful of websites on the internet and the vast majority of people had no opportunity to touch it. Now most everybody has a cell phone and the majority of those phones are capable of accessing the internet which has millions of websites all over the world. The environment has changed dramatically and if you think your opinion doesn't matter you aren't seeing the reality of life as it is this day.

Right wing conservatives are shouting about the ills of liberals who want to tax everyone to death and establish communistic government governance to run our lives. The left wing liberals cry about the conservatives selling out to big business to break our backs and rob us blind. The divisions among us as a result of this strategy of divide and conquer during election seasons in the past ten years has made me sick. It is a form of mass hysteria and just as any mass hysteria is usually founded upon unrealistic ideas and perpetuated by extremist leaders. These people are no better than the religious extremists who want to bomb buildings and kill infidels. It's the same poison with a different flavor. The only solution is to empower the individual to think and act on their own understanding of the world through a realistic perspective which holds the potential to create solutions take actions towards positive and constructive ends through positive and constructive means. Most people, even politicians regardless of their particular views are honest, hardworking and their intentions are genuinely good. There are no veiled agenda of sleeper cell or Manchurian candidate or conspiracies as has been suggested by the right wing and most right wing types are genuinely concerned about something that should be feared; totalitarianism and communism. They are both right for the reasons they fear what they fear and have good reason to fear the things they fear. The problem is they are driven to action by fear instead of a realistic perspective of the world as it is. They are out of touch with reality and fail to see the third side to the story; the truth. They are so focused and so intent on their own ideas that they overreact and sensationalize every detail to the point thy make mountains out of pebbles and fail to see the real mountains that need to be moved. They perpetuate fear which is the impetus of anger, hatred, mass hysteria and extremist action. It's not that they are evil; they are just average people trying to do an extraordinary job.

Before you accept a point of view and perpetuate it, you would be wise to examine it and do some research of your own, consider other perspectives and test your logic. Think for yourself and you'll likely find yourself with a point of view that likes and dislikes some things on the right and some things on the left. Don't be quick to dismiss a point of view offered by anyone as even the most twisted and cynical points of view when examined and contemplated can at the very least help you find another point of logic as you attempt to form an argument. Diamonds which are the most precious, brilliant and beautiful things in the world are found in dirty nasty coal pits, so even the worst ideas and the most disgusting bits of humanity can generate something valuable if we dig through them. Listen to it, take it in, study it dissect it measure it and see what you come up with based upon your own experience; you might be surprised, even delighted with what you find. Most people are focused and motivated upon the ends to a thing; "the ends justify the means", but the greater truth can be found in the means. We all have decisions to make and actions to take and it's not always easy to know what the right thing to do is especially when we worry about the outcome and use it as the measure of what the right thing should be. The truth is that you don't have control over the outcome because there are always factors which you have no control over. All you can do is your best to do what you think is right and leave the rest of the thing; the outcome, to God or fate or whatever you want to deem it. Think about it from the perspective of if you had it to do over again even if it didn't work out I would take the same action because it is the right thing to do. If the outcome isn't what you expected your lesson for the next time shouldn't be to act differently or fail to act at all just because it didn't work out the way you wanted the time before. If your actions were wrong and caused a thing to fail then by all means adjust your strategy for success, but if it I going to cost something to someone else then it shouldn't be done without their input. This is a difficult point for me to make as it is difficult to explain it in a way which is clear and concise and easily understood. Maybe a good example would be voting. Just because the person or thing you voted for didn't win the election doesn't mean you should have voted differently. You shouldn't vote for the winner, you should vote for what you believe is right based upon a clear knowledge and understanding of the thing. It's the same thing with every decision; you take the information you have at the time and do the best you can based upon the circumstances as you understand them.

BTW: If you are at the poll to vote and there is an item on the ballot you aren't educated about you should probably not vote on the matter thereby allowing those who are knowledgeable of the matter to decide the best outcome of the thing. Get educated about the issues before you get there and don't rely on the opinions of others to determine your point of view; think for yourself. I'm not saying to ignore the opinions of others because it is wise to listen to any point of view you can find and take in as much information as possible even if you disagree with it; take it in, apply the facts and logic to weigh it and then form your own opinion. If everybody would get educated about the issues and everybody would vote, our country and our world would be a far better place.

DEATH AND OTHER CIRCUMSTANCES

Death is a natural part of life and there are a multitude of various circumstances which may present themselves throughout life. Very few circumstances in life are accidental and very few can be attributed to an act of God. A true accident is a happening which is uncontrollable, unavoidable and unforeseeable and is therefore the only circumstance you can attribute to be an act of God. A true act of God is something which has no discernable matter of fact of knowledge to explain it. The word "accident" is used too often in reference to things which aren't accidents.

A helicopter is flying at 5000 feet above the ground with several passengers and even though it has been thoroughly inspected and well maintained a part in the engine fails and sends the bird crashing to the ground and killing everyone in it; this is an accident. Although, if it is later discovered that the failing part was manufactured in a defective manner or was a bad design then the crash is no longer an accident; it is the result of a choice of action of human beings who designed and built the part. Even if they didn't know prior to the crash of any other way to make the part better and it isn't discovered for ten years that there is a better way to make it, the crash is still not an accident or an act of God.

Of course people want their illusions and so at the funeral they say things like he was so special and God wanted him because he was so perfect. No. He died in a helicopter crash because of a defective part which was made by people and God really had no hand in what happened. This example is just to highlight a thing I see every day in life that I find disturbing. We want to assign responsibility for everything to God instead of taking responsibility for what is in our hands to do. When I see a person drop dead and there is no explanation from any medical reason; he is perfectly healthy and there is no reason to be found for why he died then I will say God did it. Let's get real and stop pretending that God is running every little nuance of our lives so we can start taking action from our hands to do what is right. Let's start living in the real world where the actions of people and other organisms have consequences. If you get sick it isn't God's fault; it is the result of an organism which has infected you or a condition in your body which is the result of lifestyle and genetic factors; there is nothing mystical about it. The weather isn't an act of God; it is the result of the happenings in the atmosphere regarding the sun, wind, dirt and moisture. God didn't whip up a tornado to knock down that trailer park. A police officer or firefighter dies in the line of duty because that is the nature of those jobs; they are dangerous occupations, but it is the actions of others which causes the loss of life. Even though one may find themselves compelled to serve in these occupations as their service to God it doesn't mean they died because it was the day God appointed for them to die. On the other end of the spectrum we have the witches or astrology or psychic readings trying to predict the future for us. If God had a plan for everything in the first place what makes you think he would let you read it? What would be the point in that? It is this natural curiosity within each of us to know why; to know and to understand. The problem is we are creating a false reason for why these things happen instead of dealing with them realistically. I don't know why people would want to do this as it seems to make sense to me that if I want to know and understand something it should be the truth and not some myth I make to answer the question. As children we created mythology out of our lack of understanding of how or why a thing like thunder happens and we imagined God is bowling a few frames as a means to lessen our fears. So it seems to me that this habit of assigning responsibility to God for every circumstance we don't want to deal with is a sort of obsessive compulsive disorder in that we are stuck in this childlike state of creating a mythology to assuage our fears of death and circumstances we don't understand. So it is therefore an action or idea created out of fear. I have already addressed the issue of fear but I will be happy to explain it again.

All actions created out of fear are usually quite useless and are nothing more than forms of panic. You can't attribute a circumstance to be an act of God and then on the other hand honestly expect to hold someone else accountable. For example a case of murder or negligent homicide is a result of actions taken by a person which result in the death of another. If it was God's decision for this person to die then how can you reasonably try and convict a person for the crime? That would seem to be defiant to the will of God. If a bunch of people get cancer because their water has been tainted with some chemical then how do we hold the company of people who dumped it in the water accountable when people are dying of cancer if these illnesses and deaths were the will of God?

Let's start taking a better look around and assigning things to what they belong or as Jesus said; "Render unto Caesar what is Caesar's.".

IT'S NOT MUCH OF A LIFE,
BUT IT IS MINE

My earliest memory is of pain. I cannot remember anything before this one moment in my life when I was about five years old. I woke up this morning lying on the cold tile covered concrete floor of my bedroom. I had a sharp pain in my shoulder and my eyes were stuck shut by dried mucus. I had rolled out of bed and when I hit the floor I dislocated my collarbone. I did what any child in this circumstance does; I cried for my mom. I don't know why this is as far back as my memory goes and I mean it to say that even at that age I realized that I had no recollections of any time before this day. It has always been a puzzle to me. I can't explain this point well enough here; when I was five I wondered why it was that I couldn't remember anything prior to this day. I don't know if anyone else has noted this about their own life because I never asked anyone. Maybe it is perfectly normal, but for me it is as if who I am didn't exist before this moment. It is as if prior to this point in time I didn't exist except as a body with no soul. I knew who my Mom and Dad were of course and knew every other thing a five-year old knows, but until this moment it seems I wasn't self-aware.

Mom wasn't working at the time and was pretty much a stay at home mother and my first teacher. We would spend a little bit of time everyday practicing reading and writing skills, but it wasn't much time at all; maybe an hour and a half a day. I don't ever remember not being able to read and was always a very fast and efficient reader.

Then one day Mom had to go to work. The economy was changing and not for the better. The meat packing plant where Dad worked was shutting down. Grampa retired from the Gas Company and that created an opening which Dad was fortunate enough to get hired to fill; he's been there over thirty years now. Mom is working now and so I had to go to school. I started kindergarten and it was alright. It seemed to me that I was well ahead of my classmates in knowledge, but a little lapse in social skills. I had a hard time adjusting to the all-day work schedule that school required. I was accustomed to playing most of the day and examining everything for myself and especially in daydreaming. These things got me into trouble on a daily basis and it was quite regular for me to be going to the principals' office for a spanking. I was a standout as a child for these reasons and the teachers had a hard time keeping my attention. Today we would try to put this child on some sort of medication to control their behavior. Attention deficit is no disorder! It is a natural state of the human animal and is quite necessary for learning and adapting to one's environment. It is a survival mechanism!

I don't remember why but I had to start riding the bus home from school. I suppose it was useful to save time and energy for Mom. The bus dropped me off two blocks away from home and the trip home from the bus stop was up a steep hill. There were some boys who lived closer to the bus stop who didn't like me. They were the local bullies and I wasn't respecting their authority so they decided they would put me in my place. Most every day on that bus stop as the bus pulled away I got jumped and beaten by no less than five boys who were all no less than a year older than me. I was a skinny kid and most of them were bigger and stronger than me. I tried to run away but they could catch me easily if I ran up the hill towards home. I tried that a few times and then I tried running the flat street away from the stop. It would add two blocks to my trip home but I thought if I could get a big enough of a lead they would give up chasing. I was wrong they caught me within a block and the beating was worse for making them chase me. The last time I tried to run from them I ran down the hill. They caught me after about three blocks and gave me my beating. I was tired and in pain and had to limp my way home for five blocks; I'd had enough. My Mom didn't know what to do about it I guess. I would come home with a bloody lip or nose and she would clean me up and soon enough it was forgotten I suppose. I know she told my Dad what was going on when he got home, but he was usually too drunk to care to do anything about it.

Having no choice but to fight my own battle I did what any cornered animal does; I got nasty. My Dad for his part took opportunities to push me around when he came home drunk. I developed an intense hatred for injustice as I watched my drunken father dominate and abuse my mother and suffered my own sort of injustice at school and on the bus stop. It was a normal of south St. Joseph for boys to exhibit a sort of tough guy image, even though most of them even to this day won't take any action or run their mouth without having someone outnumbered. It is this sort of gutlessness only helped to drive my rage in those bus stop fights. A neighbor kid I used to play; Kyle, and his older Brother Ronnie helped to provide some sort of martial arts training for me, free of charge. Kyle and I would square off from time to time while Ronnie and his friends watched. It served as some sort of entertainment to a certain extent, but for the most part Ronnie who was the man of the house genuinely wanted to toughen his Brother up and I was a good practice dummy because I wouldn't quit. We would beat the snot out of each other and experimented with every tactic we could think of and some Ronnie would throw in, but it was safer than the bus stop because we were already home and we had a referee. This is where I would develop the skills I needed to win on the bus stop. My older Brother David wasn't around much. He lived with his Mom and only came to visit once or twice a month if that. I got an idea from him to pick one of these guys that were jumping me on the bus stop and make his life hell until he stopped participating. So I would pick one guy and I would let him know as soon as I saw him at school that if he showed up for that fight I was going to beat the snot out of him. I would make remarks to him about it all day and on the bus ride home. When the bus pulled away I would lock onto him and give him everything I had with no regard for the other guys who were beating on me. Pretty soon five boys became four and then three and finally by the spring of my third grade year it was down to two.

After spending all that time practicing and fighting three and four, fighting two wasn't much of a challenge. I beat one of those boys so badly that he didn't go to school the next day. His cousin wanted revenge for the pummeling I had given both of them. I didn't say anything to him all day or even on the bus ride home. He gave me no indication he was going to do anything. I figured he wouldn't do anything because he didn't have help so I wasn't expecting it when he didn't wait for the bus to pull away; he jumped straight down the stairs and tackled me. He had me locked down in half-guard; pinned on my side with my right arm under me, he grabbed hold of my hair and began slamming my head into the sidewalk like he was trying to crack it open. I had been afraid before when fighting these boys but this time it was different, I was afraid for my life and felt an explosion of rage from within myself and I wanted to kill him. The whole thing was planned apparently with some adult involvement because just across the street watching and laughing was the other boy who stayed home and his mother and brothers. They were laughing alright until I got my right arm wiggled free from under me free and knocked the piss out of this kid, got up and kicked him in the gut a couple of times. I marched straight up the street to the alleyway and found a beer bottle, picked it up cracked it open on the sidewalk and began marching down the street towards the boy who had just tried to kill me. I was determined to send a message that if they were going to be so brutal, if they could hate me enough to try to kill me, then I could play the game by their rules and be just as nasty. Of course the bus driver stopped me, but the message had been sent anyway. I wanted to not only win this fight, but win every other fight afterward by instilling so much fear in not only this boy but any other boy who might want to try me, thereby winning those fights without fighting at all; I had every intention of using that broken bottle. All I ever wanted was for them to leave me alone and if I had to kill one of them to make my point, then so be it.

After school the next day the principal called my parents in to discuss the matter. My parents argued about it when we got home. Dad was bitching at Mom for not letting him know what was going on, but Mom argued back that she'd told him and if he wasn't drunk all the time he'd have done something about it by now. My Dad went down to the house where those kids lived, knocked on the door, asked for their Dad and let him know that if his boys laid a hand on me again that he would be back to beat him senseless. It was a great relief to me to have my Dad do that. It was probably the first time I felt like he really cared for me at all. I was a nine year old kid who had been pushed to the point I wanted to kill someone. My parents decided to move soon after this; I believe they hoped a change of scenery would find some peace for their son before he ended up getting seriously hurt or seriously hurt someone else, but the damage was already done; I had opened Pandora's' box so to speak. I had tapped into the evil within myself. I had found a part of me that I hated, but realized I needed. I never feared getting hurt myself as much as I feared the potential that I could lose control and hurt someone else to a point which doesn't heal with time. This incident was the first in a series of acute incidents I would experience growing up. The struggle had begun when the fighting first began; the struggle to hold in the pain and bury it. The problem with pushing these things down into yourself and not standing up for yourself is two-fold. First those who push you get the idea that you are weak and won't fight back and bullies like to target those who can't hurt them because they feel weak and afraid. Secondly, eventually it builds to a point of critical mass as you fight your own natural desire to exert yourself upon your world and all it takes is one spark to ignite the fire. I'm not certain if you could truly define these incidents as temporary insanity. Though to the observer I seemed out of control and apparently unable to reason against the wrong of desiring to do serious harm to another human being, but as far as I know based upon the legal definition people who find themselves in such a state don't realize it or don't recall it quite as vividly. This was not the case with me however; I was in what seemed to me a very lucid state. I realized that I had the opportunity to get the upper hand in the situation and I was very calculating and precise in my actions. The only thing that seemed out of control about me was the need to exert energy; to take all the anger I had bottled up and release it upon something and only the person or persons who had ignited it seemed to be the logical choice of targets.

We moved east of St. Joseph, into the country, on a farm near Clarksdale. The fourth grade was fairly peaceful for me. Of course there were the dominant boys who tried to let the new kid know they were to be respected but I didn't kiss anybody's ass. I didn't have to fight them; I just let them know I wasn't going to be pushed around. The school at Clarksdale shut down after my fourth grade year and we had to be bused to Maysville for school. The bus ride was more than an hour long and since the Maysville School included junior high and high school I had to ride the bus with these older kids. That is how I met my next nemesis. This boy who was in high school and I had a fight on a regular basis over a seat on the bus. It all started because he was a bully and liked to push the younger kids around and I hated bullies. I usually got on the bus before he did after school and I wanted to sit at the back of the bus in his favorite seat. He and the other high school kids thought those seats should be reserved for them and I wanted to antagonize him. It worked out pretty good for me because since I was able to hold my own against a boy who was twice my size nobody at that school wanted to mess with me. The last time we fought he slammed my head into the window post and I lost it and it took four other high school boys to pull me off of him. Until that point it had just been some poking and shoving and some wrestling, but this time I was out to send a message again. I didn't want to kill anybody this time but I certainly wanted to give him some pain that would last for a couple of days at least so he'd have something to think about.

We moved again back to St. Joseph to the old house in the south end for a year so that Mom and Dad could save up a down payment on a house in Savannah. My year in the 7th grade was no different from the years before during grade school. I had my first fight after the first day of school. A boy who had previously been one of my best friends in elementary school was talking to a girl while we were waiting on the bus to take us home for the day saying that he could whip my ass and I disagreed without hesitation so we set a time for the fight that afternoon. When we showed up for the fight I pleaded with him to reconsider and remember that we had once been good friends but he would have none of it. He insulted my mother and as usual in that neighborhood if someone said "Your mama" if you didn't throw down you were a punk. I decided I was going to not only win this fight but also send a message to potential challengers. He came to school the next day with the whole left side of his head severely bruised. Of course he tried to lie about it and claimed I had hit him with a board and I made it perfectly clear to him and the other boys who had been there to witness the fight were going to lie about it and impugn my honor then I was going to have to beat the snot out of all of them to prove my point and they changed their tune. The consolidation of several grade schools into the Spring Garden Middle School building created the opportunity to interact with boys I hadn't known in grade school. The opportunity to learn new methods in the application of pain and the formation of my belief in natural selection; I believed I was superior. It was sort of my Alpha male attitudinal phase in early puberty.

When we moved to Savannah a year later my father made it perfectly clear that getting into a fight with one boy in Savannah would only lead to the need to fight all their friends. So what is new about that Dad? My freshman year of high school I had a few incidents with upper classman that ended favorably for me; not that I whipped anyone's ass really but I earned respect for my willingness to stand up for myself and at least proved I could take the hits and hit back. So challengers were few and far between after that, but I didn't have many social options though because of the way I operated. My sophomore year my Brother David moved in with us. David had moved around allot growing up and because of this he had allot of fights being the new kid at school all the time. As kids my Brother and I spent summers together and allot of time practicing martial arts. We studied everything we could find in books and movies and video games. We saw it and then went out in the yard and practiced it. David and I would fight full speed quite often just for fun. We cut up broom handles to make upchucks and beat the snot out of each other on a regular basis. My Brother David was the best and dearest friend I have ever had and nobody ever had a better brother. He never waned in his duty as a brother to make me strong, challenge my intellect, protect me from harm if necessary and to occasionally kick my ass if I needed it. Despite the negative aspects of his drug use he was everything a brother should be; no one will ever have a better brother.

There was one incident my sophomore year of high school when I kicked in a heavy ventilation grate in the hallway at school when a good friend of mine had pushed me against a wall onto a light switch. The sharp pain to my spine instantly set me off, but I was primed for it as I was having a really bad day being pushed around by some upper class students. I had to release the energy but this was the first time I think that I was able to refrain from taking it out on another person and managed to get through it without having to be restrained by others. I didn't want to hurt my friend and all I could do to restrain myself was to walk out of the class room and put my foot into that grate. I kept going down the hall and sat down on the floor in front of my locker and cried. The vice- principal found me a few minutes later and took me to his office to talk about the incident. I cried during fights when I would find myself getting angry; not outright bawling but I would shed tears. It was because I was afraid of what I might do. I was fighting back the urge to let go and let the evil take over and I was afraid of losing control. Of course the other boys would laugh at me for this and my only response was to tell them that they don't understand.

Needless to say this became a sort of way of life for me to a certain extent and I became rooted in the belief that all I was good at had to do with fighting. I couldn't see any other potential in myself for anything good. I despised violence, but it was the only thing I thought I was good at. Then I discovered literature and the arts, thanks to my Brother David, and found I had a new potential that seemed natural. When I got into high school I discovered I had a pretty good head for business and social studies and found my personal disgust for injustice easily spilled over into the concerns of the world. My biggest opportunity in developing my ability to assert myself was and probably is in my habit of being a little too honest for the tastes of most people. I've gotten better over the years at containing my desire to just blurt out what I think but from time to time it manages to get me on someone's bad side.

I learned growing up in an alcohol fueled home of violence to keep my armor tight. I kept my relationships with people cold and distant. I watched everyone around me and grew eyes in the back of my head. I was paranoid of everyone. It's why I had a hard time finding acceptance in my peer groups. They were afraid of me because I was quiet and didn't understand me and I was afraid of them because they would only seek to hurt me if I let them in. So began the life of mutual disregard I have lived for until a short time ago.

My birthday is February 10. In 2009 my birthday was on a Tuesday and the following Saturday was Valentine's Day. I tried to get a couple of friends to help me celebrate my birthday at Power and Light in Kansas City and of course Saturday was my only day off, but I ended up being there alone with nobody I know to care for me. My birthday and Valentine's Day I was alone. My Mom is gone so she wasn't here to tell me happy birthday, my Brother David is dead too and no one else seemed to care. I have felt alone my whole life, but I had learned to accept it as just the way it is. But on that night it began to bother me. I began to wonder what the point in living was if I am alone and have no one to share my life with. I wasn't thinking about suicide, I was simply arguing with myself. I thought about all the times in my life I had traveled somewhere and how it was never really fun because I was alone. No one calls, no one comes by so it is logical to conclude that no one really cares for me because if they did they would think about me and be compelled to contact me and interact with me. I don't blame them because I didn't like being around me either. I really put a lot of time into these thoughts and began redesigning my behavior concerning my interactions with other people. Many of them were really put off by the change in my behavior as it was odd to them to find me behaving in this new manner and so they were probably a bit suspicious of me and weren't readily accepting of this change even though it was a good thing. So it wasn't easy to do right away. There were days when it was frustrating and I wanted to naturally revert to my old ways but I kept going and believing and as time went on it became easier and then it became the norm and started paying off.

I am a single parent of an eleven year old boy who is the sweetest kid a parent could ever have. I quit college 4 years ago to take care of my Mom while she was dying of cancer and went to work full time as a welder and heavy equipment operator. I made excellent income and though nothing of the meager 25% of it I was throwing away on the bills to buy a couple of new cars and a motorcycle and other things. Now with the economy the way it is I had been working my ass off at 3 jobs combining for over 65 hours every week and still make less than 30% of what I made sitting in the cab of an excavator which has given me no other alternative but to file bankruptcy.

The point is that I am on my ass as badly as I could be but somehow I have found the peace within myself that I have been searching for my whole life. I have achieved a point of enlightenment in my life and have finally starting to become the man I always wanted to be. I don't get angry anymore because I am not afraid. I am reaching out to others in my life and genuinely trying to show them compassion and find that I care very deeply for them and they are responding positively, yet I am not afraid of the possibility that they will reject me. I have no desire to control anyone else; I have no demands or expectations of anyone, only hope. I have shed my armor and have found the greatest warrior within myself.

I am reminded of a man who lived in feudal Japan a long time ago who is considered to be the greatest samurai swordsman of all time. As a young man he fought and won his first duel at the age of 13; to win was to kill your opponent. By the time he was 27 he had killed dozens of swordsman in duels and he realized there was no honor in it because there is no honor in the strong overcoming the weak. He concluded the only honor was to be found in defeating his opponents while sparing their lives. He never took another life, won hundreds more duels; using a wooden sword, and lived to 80 some years of age. It is said he even developed a technique to fight against and disarm a swordsman with an imaginary sword.

Anger, frustration, confrontation, antagonism and rage are simply modes of panic. Panic is the common response to fear. Panic is the inability to think creatively to solve a problem. A good example is the video game analogy; when you panic, you lose the ability to come up with a logical solution so you begin flailing around, slapping buttons in hopes of getting lucky. Panic is a strange contradiction. Our fear is caused by a lack of control over the circumstances or people we are faced with which are uncontrollable to begin with and our response is to discard the one thing we can control which is the only thing which can be of help to us; ourselves. All I can control is how I act. Anyone who says they simply lost control is not being honest. No one loses control really; they give up control. I am not saying it is easy, but it is simple. Catching yourself when you begin to get angry or frustrated (panic) and recognizing that if you give up yourself then there is nothing you can do to make things better for yourself or for others. There is nothing good to be found in forcing your way through with anger and aggression. Even if you succeed in your task you lose and so do the other people involved. Anger is like armor. When you're faced with a fight, you the warrior are compelled to tighten up your armor and prepare for battle, but realizing that you are much more agile without your armor and can better deflect the blows that come at you without that armor, makes you the greater warrior. The greatest warrior needs no armor.

It was my Dad's discovery of his alcoholism and realization of the dysfunction of my rearing which truly began my journey towards self-actualization. I was seventeen when my Dad got sober and I had to figure out for myself what it implied for me. I wondered if I would end up being an alcoholic myself. I saw my Brother David's drug addiction destroying him and his mind and my Brother Michael's sex addiction and drug use getting him into trouble with the law. David was and is the most intelligent person I have ever met. It was profoundly disturbing for me to lose him in the fall of 2000 to suicide. His drug abuse had damaged his brain to the point he had become schizophrenic I guess or maybe his drug addiction was a result of his mental disease; no one can really say. All I know is no one has had or ever will have a better brother. From what I know of the circumstances surrounding his death it is clear to me that he sacrificed his life to save mine; the voices were compelling him to kill his little Brother based upon some Cane and Abel scenario. Losing David was devastating to me and I did go through a period of profound depression. I would stay up all night grinding away with pencil and paper writing down every thought that was flowing through my head. I wrote hundreds of pages of poems and essays and ideas about a multitude of things. He was the best friend I will ever have with the exception of my Mom.

Gone Home

He's here somewhere in the dark, watching me, whispering his secrets beneath the lies.

Answers he never a question and knowing all the truth I need.

The shadow of the Magician of Color and Light, waiting in torment for something of me.

Waiting for me to set him free, but I don't know how to let him go or why he thinks I don't need him so.

I've imprisoned the soul that I love the most, as all I have left of him is a ghost, who haunts my mind, dreams and imagination.

My Brother, best friend and life's inspiration.

As I burn this flax to ease my pain and piss my life down the drain, through another day without light and burning eyes of tear filled sight, I too become a ghost.

Lost my Brother to a broken heart, lost my mind and fell apart.

No relief in the tears I cry, no relief in the lies I lied.

I don't know why the magician is gone, the way he left had to be wrong,

How to express, the means I lack and nothing I do will bring him back.

There is no way to give this riddle sense and I cannot stop the suicide already dispensed.

My only hope and all I can say: he's gone home, home to stay.

There is no way I can explain to lessen my suffering or ease the pain.

I don't want to talk about it anymore or ponder the "why" and "what for".

I want to cut myself open and pour it all out, I want to explode, scream and shout.

I'm lost in denial and thinking "what ifs" and trying to find the truth in the myths.

I went into shock, emotional shutdown as the body of David was laid in the ground.

My dearest Brother and only true friend, till the end of my life will I see him again.

All I can do with this emptiness I find is to fill it with the broken pieces he left behind.

As I lay down these words to fill this page, I find my heart in such a rage.

I'm running out of words to express and explain, with no one but the paper to hear me complain.

When I run out of words this song must end as I'm left in silence still missing my friend.

I can't hold on anymore, but I can't let go, having these questions to the answers he knows.

I wish I could have him for one more day, but it wouldn't be enough for me anyway, wouldn't be enough for me to say goodbye, I'd miss him the same till the day I die.

My only hope and all I can say: he's gone home, home to stay.

My Mom passed away from lung cancer at the age of 53 just three years ago. I quit college to try to take care of her and watched her suffer for a year and a half. Losing the two closest people to me has had a profound impact upon me. It has made me realize how terrible a thing it is to waste my potential to do all that I can do to become all that I can be.

Six

Six months they say, and never any more
Six months isn't much, but it puts me on the floor

Six months and you'll be gone, you leave me
To think that you'll be gone, no! Can't be!

There's never enough time in each and every day
Never enough time to express what I need to say

The days roll by and soon you're gone from me
Six months from now, you'll be gone you see

It hurts too much that I don't have the time
It hurts...oh so much...but I don't have the time

No time to pause or even slow down
Have no time and no time for being down

I don't have time to spend on you before you leave
I don't have time after you go, to stop and grieve

I love you Mom is all I have to say
I love you Mom is all I can say

I have just recently made it back to college. I am a single Dad of the most wonderful son a parent ever had. My son is different from me when I was a child in a lot of ways but similar in enough to make me a little nervous. Like any parent I want him to have all the opportunities to be all he can be that I didn't have. Being a child of a single parent is a bad hand to be dealt to him though and I worry about the implications. I try to teach him to appreciate what he has and not worry too much about what he doesn't have; for the most part he's pretty good with it. He is very smart and good at a lot of things I don't think I was very good at when I was his age. He has had a couple of run-ins with bullies when he was five or six had to fight a time or two and handled it well, though he had some difficulty accepting his need to assert himself in this manner. I had to explain to him how it is necessary to defend yourself when you are attacked and it is perfectly alright to do so and yes if it happens at school there may be consequences; it's just part of the game. For the most part he manages to get along pretty good and doesn't have any trouble really. He is strongly independent just as I have taught him to be. He maintains the same kind of detachment with people that I see in myself and other self-actualizing people in that he won't put up with people who treat others unfairly. It's my belief that he has all the potential to be a much better man than I could ever be and maybe he already is. I'm not a perfect parent of course. I have had my moments of frustration and made mistakes in dealing with him, but I never hesitate to apologize to him when I realize I was wrong and explain to him why I was wrong.

People often accuse me of over analyzing things but I find great insight in things that most people find to be mundane and average or don't even notice at all. I don't analyze things to make them more complicated, I am stripping away the parts and pieces and getting to the root of the issue; I'm simplifying them. I can always find something beautiful almost anywhere anytime I feel like looking, so I try to make a habit of it. It could be as simple as noticing some flowers and really taking a good look at them; someone went through the trouble to plant them and care for them so they could grow so the least I could do is to take a moment to appreciate something someone wanted to share. I think it is a point of connecting with this other person, even if I never meet them I have received a piece of them they left for me to find. It's kind of rude to not notice them I think. It's the same when someone speaks up to offer a perspective. Whether I agree with it or not, I still try to listen and hear them out before jumping to any conclusion or trying to argue with them and most of the time I just ask questions which cause them to challenge their point of view for themselves. I don't just say that is wrong and this I right; that I the worst kind of argument as it fails to offer a person the chance to examine a thing for themselves. It kind goes back to that culture-diffusion idea I mentioned earlier. If you have a different view than my view then by all means share it with me please; don't leave me to my ignorance.

I'm no better and no worse than anyone else who has ever lived. We all have the same opportunity to be wrong or right, good or evil in our actions. We are all perfectly imperfect in that we all have the perfect power to be everything anyone could ever be whether it be good or bad. Good or bad is just a matter of perspective and if there was a day when the majority of society determined to be good an act we now think to be evil then it' status has changed as the perspective has changed. Every idea which is manifest into the world begins in one moment with one being to determine its value and drive it to existence and even the worst results can begin with the best of intentions. Feelings, thoughts and words are meaningless without actions which prove them.

SOME RANDOM THOUGHTS ALONG THE WAY

I am a reflection of my society. I want money, just like the rest of my society; money and material to validate my existence; validate my voice. I want my voice and fifteen minutes to make my mark. Voice has a price; money. You can be the richest person in the world and even if the words you speak are nothing but vain and meaningless dribble, you are heard and your worthless words immortalized in a media circus, while the poor poet with a golden tongue who speaks of the bread of life is just a whisper in the darkness of an empty meadow; no one cares, no one listens. He is a ghost which doesn't even cast a shadow on the ground where he stands

WORTHLESS ME

The value of myself and my worthless life; I found confidence in the things I do. Reaching out to lend a hand to another, only to find that my good deeds mean nothing to anyone but me. As I searched for my value in the will of the other to which my works matter not, I found that I matter not; I became nothing and no one. I did what I did for others to validate who I am. I found myself with no friends to consume my time; only my thoughts. I thought I think too much. So I tried to think of a way to stop thinking so much, but I had too much time to think about what a waste my thoughts amounted to. Eventually I came to the thought and the realization that my true motive wasn't to fulfill the pleasure of others through my works but rather my own pleasure. I discovered that it means something to me; it pleases me. In realizing this I realized a deeper truth to my existence which is to find validation of myself from myself. Acting upon this motivation I am acting in true form of love as I am giving with no concern of return on what I give. Giving with the desire for a return is an investment. Giving without regard for return out of the purity of giving is a gift, even if it is for the self-serving reason of self-validation.

One day some years ago when I was about twelve while squirrel hunting a strange and wonderful thing happened that had a profoundly positive effect on me. I was sitting on a log I had sat on dozens of times before being quiet waiting for a squirrel to come along and I was approached by a doe and her fawn. Thy came right up to me, face-to-face within arms' reach and looked me up and down real good for a minute before calmly moving along on their way. I thought it was amazing they hadn't been afraid of me and came so close to me. A few years later when I was deer hunting I was practicing walking or rather moving through the timber like a deer rather than a man as my Brother David had taught me so that I could sneak up on a deer. I was following a deer trail and eventually I came upon a doe. I didn't have a doe tag so I wasn't going to shoot her, but I wanted to see if it was really going to work and find out how close I could get to her. I walked right up to her ever so easily and came face-to-face with her within arm's reach and she didn't seem at all nervous despite the fact it was the middle of deer season. I gave her a few seconds before whispering "BOO!" at which point she ran off. She didn't fear me because she thought I was just another deer. She didn't judge me by how many legs I had or anything that had to do with what I looked like. She had simply judged me by the character which I had presented to her; I acted like a deer and so she treated me like a deer. I thought about this a lot and relate it to the perspective of Martin Luther King Jr. when he spoke of his dream of a world where we would judge one another by our character instead of what we look like. Take it as far as you can and you can think of it not only from the perspective of race but also any other potential characteristic which may serve to divert you away from interacting with others. Even the bum in the alley or down by the river can have something you could learn from or appreciate.

Pull the bricks out of your wall for a minute and try to appreciate something around you. Just contemplate the beauty of something for a minute and get a natural high from it; these are my pills. It is a moment in time that will pass and you will probably forget it before the day is over but it has the power to make a positive adjustment to your perspective which can perpetuate throughout your day and to those you interact with. I like to take pictures of these little moments and have recently begun loading them up on Facebook to share them with others. I find I have a better day when I take a moment to notice the sunrise and appreciate the start of a new day. It relaxes me to catch a glimpse of the sunset and take a moment to breathe and evaluate my day and focus on what I accomplished. We all have days when it is hard to see what we did. We get so busy and it seems like there isn't enough time in the day to get the things we need to do done and even less time to do anything we want to do, but just taking a moment to step aside from the hassles of everyday life and reconnect with your soul make a huge difference. I have laid on the ground on a clear and starry night, felt the rumbling Earth barreling through the cosmos and find I'm connected to the whole universe and it is good.

I'm reminded of the original Pink Floyd *The Wall* video; the journey of a person into a world of his own design. He lives behind his wall separated and protected from the rest of humanity as a means of defending their individuality; yet they remain divided against themselves as they are torn from the part of themselves that needs to give and receive from others. They look for help from some pill or other drug to cope with the pain; to keep going along numb to the conditions and reality of life. We are shown through his experience and see how as a youth the individual is stripped away from a person and they find themselves just another shapeless indistinguishable face in the crowd. In the end we find him being judged by a court of his own mind and resolves to tear down the wall. It is the natural desire to preserve our individuality, to become what we are we have turned against ourselves out of fear. Don't trudge through your life afraid to dream and afraid to act upon those dreams. We all possess great potential to do great things; believe in yourself and while you're at it believe in someone else even when they are having a hard time believing in themselves.

I still don't know for certain what I will do with myself. I still don't know for certain where I am going in life or what I am going to do with my potential. The only thing I know is that I want to do some great things to make the world a better place just as I have always wanted; I still don't know exactly what that will be, maybe politics. For now I have some other projects I want to work on which I believe hold the potential to change the world in ways I haven't completely analyzed but have imagined fairly well. The potential success of this book will definitely change my life in respect to these goals as it will provide a financial means to support these projects. Some are related to literature, some to sociology, some to international law and politics and still others to engineering, energy production, worldwide poverty as well as environmental conservation. My journey of a million miles and it all begins with this one first step.

THANK YOU

I hope that you have enjoyed the things I have shared with you in this little book. I hope that you will tell a friend about it and they will like it well enough to tell someone else. I hope that in these little pieces of me I have shared you can find something you can take and make your own. I hope it makes your day a little brighter and as a result you make the day better or those you interact with. I want to thank you so much for purchasing and reading my first attempt at realizing my dreams of becoming a published author. If you would like to express some sort of feedback whether it be praise or argument or a different perspective I welcome you to email me at infectedintellects@yahoo.com.

BIBLIOGRAPHY

Chedd, G. (Producer), & Alda, A. (Director). (2008). The Human Spark [Motion Picture]. PBS.

Beitsch, R., & Winters, N. (2009, April 10). Missouri House passes amendment allowing concealed weapons on college campuses. Retrieved July 2010, from www.columbiamissourian.com: http://www.columbiamissourian.com/packages/concealed-carry-campus/

Bloomberg, M. (2007, April 30). Newsweek, p. 47.

Burke, R. (2008). From International Rights to National Development: The First UN International Conference on Human Rights, Tehran, 1968. Journal of World History, Vol. 19, No. 3, 19(3).

Card, O. S. (1985). Ender's Game. Tor Books.

Edwards, M. S., Scott, K. M., Allen, S. H., & Irvin, K. (2008). Sins of Commision? Understanding membership patterns on the United Nations Human Rights Commision. Political Research Quarterly, Vol. 61(No. 390).

Goodman, R., & Jinks, D. (2004). How to Influence States: Socialization and International Human Rights Law. Duke Law Journal, 54.

Hafner-Burton, E. M., & Tsutsui, K. Retrieved July 2010, from Sage Journals Online: http://jpr.sagepub.com/content/44/407

Hafner-Burton, E. M., Tsutsui, K., & Meyer, J. W. (n.d.). International Human Rights Law and the Politics of Legitimization:: Repressive States and HUman Rights Treaties. Retrieved July 2010, from Sage Journals Online: http://iss.sagepub.com/content/23/1/115

Jung, Carl G. (1957). The Undiscovered Self. New American Library; Signet.

Lott, John R. Jr. (2000). When Gun Control Costs Lives. National Forum, Vol. 80(Issue 4), 29-33.

Kates, D. B., & Mauser, G. (2007). Would Banning Firearms Reduce Murder and Suicide. Harvard Journal of Law and Public, Vol. 30(Issue 2), 649-694.

Kroeber, A. L. (1940). Stimulus Diffusioon. University of Berkeley, Department of Anthropology.

Locke, J. (1689). Two Treatises of Government. Awnsham Churchill Publications.

Lucas, G., McCallum, R. (Producers), & Lucas, G. (Director). (2005). Star Wars; Episode 3: Revenge of the Sith [Motion Picture].

Malcolm, J. L. (2002, November). Gun Control's Twisted Outcome. Reason, 34(6), 20-26.

Malcolm, J. L. (n.d.). Lessons of History: Firearms Regulationa and the Reduction of Crime. Texas Review of Law and Politics, Vol. 8, 176-187.

Maslow, A. H. (1954). Motivation and Personality. Harper Press.

McDowell, D. (1995, Autumn). Easing Concealed Firearms Laws: Effects on Homicide in Three States. Journal of Criminal Law and Criminology, 86(1), 193-206.

Moorhouse, J. C., & Wanner, B. (2006). Does Gun Control Reduce Crime or Does Crime Increase Gun Control? Cato Journal, 103-124.

Neil, B., & Neil, B. (2009, February). The Heller Decision and its Possible Implications for Right-to-Carry Laws Nationally. Journal of Contemporary Criminal Justice, 25(1), 113-118.

NRA-ILA (National Rifle Association- Intsitute for Legislative Action). (2003, September 12). Missouri Overrides Governor's Veto of Right to Carry Bill! Retrieved July 2010, from www.nra-ila.org: http://www.nra-ila.org/Legisaltion/Read. aspx?id=824

NRA-ILA (National Rifle Association-Intsitute for Legislative Action). (2010, June 6). Right to Carry 2010. Retrieved July 2010, from www.nra-ila.org: http://www.nra-ila.org/Issues/ Factsheets/Read.aspx?id=18&issue=003

Risse, T., & Sikkink, K. (1998). The Power of Human Rights: International Norms and Domestic Change. Cambridge University Press.

Waters, R., Marshall, A., & Parker, A. (Producers). (n.d.). The Wall [Motion Picture]. Warner Bros. (2010-present).

Wright, J. D. (1988). Second Thoughts About Gun Control. Public Interest(Issue 91), 23-39.